Building Bridges for Women of Color in Higher Education

A Practical Guide for Success

Edited by Conchita Y. Battle and Chontrese M. Doswell

University Press of America,® Inc.
Dallas · Lanham · Boulder · New York · Oxford

♾™ The paper used in this publication meets the minimum
requirements of American National Standard for Information
Sciences—Permanence of Paper for Printed Library Materials,
ANSI Z39.48—1984

This book is dedicated to all of the mentors that are building the bridges for women of color to succeed in higher education.

Table of Contents

CHAPTER 2

CHAPTER 3

List of Tables

List of Charts

Foreword

Dr. Sadie Tanner Mossell Alexander was the first African American to get a Ph.D. in economics, in 1921, when she completed her dissertation on the "Standard of Living Among One Hundred Negro Families in Philadelphia, 1916-1918" at the University of Pennsylvania. She was the first President of Delta Sigma Theta sorority, Incorporated, a social and civic leader, and one of the most important thinkers of her era. Yet she never had the opportunity to work as an academic, and one can only speculate why. Historically black colleges and universities were not necessarily woman-friendly in her era, and predominately white institutions were not open to women of color faculty in the early part of the twentieth century.

Her inability to find the kind of work that Ph.D. economists traditionally held did not prevent Alexander from becoming a societal contributor. She earned a law degree from the University of Pennsylvania in 1927, and was the first African American woman admitted to the Pennsylvania bar. She built a distinguished practice as an attorney, served on the boards of several civil rights and civic liberties organizations, and was active in politics. She and her husband, Raymond Pace Alexander, (the first African American to serve on the Philadelphia Court of Common Pleas until his death in 1974), successfully litigated numerous discrimination cases that resulted in equal access for people of color to public schools, restaurants, hotels, and theaters. They played a key role in drafting the Pennsylvania Equal Rights Law.

I have a lecture that I title, "Making Room for Sadie," in which I talk about ways that economic scholarship might have been different had Sadie Alexander had the opportunity to participate in her field of first choice. It is clear that long after she had abandoned the study of economics, Sadie Alexander remained interested in the topic, purchasing economics books into the 1950s.

In researching Sadie Alexander's life, I have developed a rich sisterly relationship with her daughter, Dr. Rae Alexander-Minter, who is Vice President of Governmental and Public Affairs at Metropolitan College of New York. In one of my conversations with Rae, she told me that I should never say anything about Sadie Alexander that would make her appear to be a victim of racism or of unfulfilled dreams or opportunities. She is right. Dr. Sadie Alexander did not only survive in the face of our nation's racism, she thrived even as she experienced bias. She thrived because of her intellect, her strength of character, her determination, and her vision. If there is any victim in Sadie Alexander's story, our nation is a victim of its myopia and limited thinking, sidelining a thinker like Sadie Alexander because of inherent biases. I agree with Rae – we shouldn't feel sorry for Sadie; we should feel sorry for a country that does not allow each individual to contribute her best to its ongoing development.

Conchita Y. Battle and Chontrese M. Doswell have produced a book that speaks to the ways we can bring new players into the higher education game, and get the best for them. It is a delight and an honor to write this forward to *Building Brides for Women of Color in Higher Education* because this book is so needed. Though we have come a long way from the days when the doors of the academy were closed to Dr. Sadie Tanner Mossell Alexander, we have not come so far as to find African American woman proportionately represented in higher education. We've come a long way from 1976, when black women earned just 1 percent of our nation's Ph.D. degrees. Even though we account for more than 60 percent of doctoral degrees earned by African Americans, we now earn just 3 percent of all doctoral degrees.

We have come a long way, baby, but we still have a long way to go, and that's why *Building Bridges* is such an important book. It provides a vital perspective of the ways that women of color survive, and even thrive, in academia, despite the stereotypes, the excessive visibility, and the discrimination that remains. It's a book I wish someone had thrust in my hands – and that of my dean and department chair – when I started out as an Assistant professor in 1980. Useful to the newcomer to academe, it is also useful affirmation and exploration for the academic veteran who, still charting her path, is interested in the ways her colleagues have developed survival strategies.

As Glenda Price, President of Marygrove College, writes in her essay, "The Accidental President", many women of color take untraditional paths to reach their positions. Roadblocks and detours are often troubling and debilitating, but equally they often remind us of the adage that when one door closes another opens. Sadie Alexander didn't have a traditional career, but she had a fruitful one. One of the messages in *Building Bridges* is to find the fruit and savor it.

Another message comes from the chapter "Wading in the Water" which speaks of slippery slopes, whirlwinds, calm waters, and anchors. The metaphors of rising tides and swirling waters abound here, as they do in earlier chapters, where AnnJanette Alejano-Steele speaks of "well chosen oars" and Emma Lucas speaks of vanguards. The message here is to hold on, to choose your path and stick to it, keeping centered even as one is barraged by conflicting messages, stormy waters, bruising waves.

Dr. Dorothy Irene Height, the President Emerita of the national Council of Negro Women often speaks of African American women "making a way out of no way." In some ways the involvement of African American women in higher education exactly reflects her sentiment that black women sail in uncharted waters, that we ride through waves instead of going around them, that we create models for ourselves because role models have hardly existed. Indeed, we create the role models that we need. We are the women for whom we have been waiting. Thus, *Building Bridges* is an eloquent statement to the power of networking, and to the ways that black women in the academy, as presidents, deans, and new assistant professors seek out sister-colleagues to help chart a successful course in higher education.

This book comes out at a critical time, a time when the role of higher education in our society is being questioned, when the role of the state in providing funding for higher education is being eroded. Increasingly, students find the playing field tilted as the financial aid universe changes, with more loans available than grants, with the tilt for new money leaning toward "merit" scholarships, not need-based ones. This book comes at a time when state universities are raising tuitions at double-digit levels, at a time when the representation of faculty of color is dropping.

African American women stakeholders in the system are called upon to act in the spirit of Anna Julia Cooper, who wrote that 'when and where I enter the interests of my race and of my gender come with me," *Building Bridges* offers African American women and other woman of color a playbook for greater effectiveness for our race and for our gender, and more broadly, it offers a perspective on ways we can make the diversity imperative work for all of us. Too, it reminds us of how far we have come since Sadie Alexander earned her Ph.D., how far we must go until we achieve parity both in numbers and in the quality of our experiences in higher education.

Foreword

I wish I could put this book in the hands of every professor, dean, provost, and president in higher education, at historically black colleges and universities and also at predominately white institutions. It is a compilation that offers insight and perspective on the "road less traveled" for women of color, and by extension, for others in higher education. Chontrese M. Doswell and Conchita Y. Battle are to be commended for opening our eyes by compiling this volume.

Julianne Malveaux, Ph.D.
Economist/Author/Commentator

Acknowledgements

I would like to thank my mother, Yvonne, and my daughter Amethyst Jai for all of their support during the process of putting this book together.

Conchita

Introduction

Building Bridges

Chontrese M. Doswell

The idea for *Building Bridges for Women of Color in Higher Education: A Practical Guide for Success* evolved from informal conversations with female, minority c olleagues. T hese c ollective c onversations, which often occurred during down time at academic conferences or over social lunches in which the topic of conversation was slated to cover anything other than academy-related issues, developed the foundation for this project. During these conversations, it became apparent that a m issing l ink or disconnect existed somewhere between the decision to pursue a terminal degree and career-path origin. For many of us, this disconnect happened while in progress with the dissertation phase of the degree. We were, in the majority of our experiences, oblivious to the fact that anything was going a rye.

Reflecting back, it makes perfect sense, not only is a prospective terminal degree holder unaware of strategic career savvy, but unaware of most other aspects of life. The dissertation is a "jealous mistress" which demands all of your attention. When a doctoral candidate is in the latter phase of the journey, they are in process towards completion around the clock either directly or indirectly. The dissertation warrior is either consciously or subconsciously in process. The processing occurs even when occupied by some another task, such as cooking dinner or cleaning the bathroom. A thought will come to mind of how to streamline the methodology or the best approach to take in guarding your territory during the next committee meeting.

A dissertation requires sacrificing many weekdays, evenings and weekends and if you have relationships with "civilians" it often means sacrificing those relationships as well. When a candidate schedules time for leisure, there is a certain amount of guilt associated with the activity because of the work that still needs to be done before completion.   It is a continuous process which is not over until the last signature is signed on the final document days after the oral defense.   The intensity of the Ph.D. process requires a candidate to continuously self- motivate and focus their attention on the task at hand.   Because of the nature of the scrutiny and the level of commitment associated with this process, the plausibility for disconnect in other areas, such as strategic career planning is completely reasonable.

Inevitably, the tenor of these discussions, which later became the inspiration for this book, would escalate to a level of frustration stemming from a source of shared experience.   The common denominator became the dearth of structures designed to promote professional development and mobility in higher education.   In other words, we were not socialized into the vocation of our chosen profession.

For many scholars, the best preparation for careers in the academy encompassed staying the course in graduate school to completion.   We felt confident that obtaining an advanced or terminal degree would ensure a certain level of career success.   Of course, while in school, we were inherently aware of the importance of conference presentations, collegial memberships, and scholarly journal publications to the academic world.   We were not, however, as astute with the broader context in which these career tools reside or the connective tissue which sustain their existence.   Over-arching strategies such as academic interviewing skills, contract negotiation skills, and conducting effective placement searches are critical to launching a successful career.   Moreover, these strategies are underscored by making the appropriate connections between career building blocks.   For example, understanding the sequential order in the path to publishing, knowing how and when to say no, or knowing how and when to ask for what you want, as well as having an awareness of the elements in a new or reinvented career which double as pitfalls.

These dynamics contribute to an illusive, political landscape.   A political culture exists in most professions and higher education is certainly no exception.   Being a person of color further complicates navigating these already murky waters.   The "perfect" edges of the landscape are maintained by the status quo.   Thus, minority women in higher education often find themselves in a precarious position.   Our mere presence chips away at the established order.   Moreover, if the extent of our political swagger encompasses only book smarts, we are at a clear disadvantage. The evolution of *Building Bridges,* therefore, was a natural progression. In fact, it did not take a lot of convincing the day my co-editor pitched the idea of collaborating on this project. Her concept was completely on point. Within minutes of our initial meeting we found ourselves finishing each other's sentences and in concert with the book's direction. A catharsis occurred, in which issues formerly allowed to remain dormant, came flooding to the surface. These were the concerns only given a voice within the context of moral support chats with colleagues. It became obvious that these concerns, cast aside as insecurities, were not assigned the importance they deserved to career promotion. When aggregated, these relegated to ancillary topics become essential to creating a competitive edge.

Building Bridges is designed to compliment the reader's competitive edge by creating a forum of collective voices from women of color in the academy. The express purpose is to provide a professional development reference guide for academicians both embarking upon and maintaining careers in higher education. The pages of this book are filled with dynamic women sharing one of their most valuable resources, the benefit of their experience. The authors mentor the reader by discussing practical lessons, mapping career path strategies, and establishing tangible time-lines for success.

The book is divided into four primary areas of higher education: (1) The Road to the Presidency: Women of Color Assuming Leadership Roles in the Academy; (2) Climate Control: Exploring the Nuances of Minority Serving Institutions and Predominately White Institutions (PWIs); (3) The Department Chair Dichotomy: Balancing Faculty and Administration; and (4) Wading in the Water: Negotiating the Faculty Tenure Process.

Chapter 1

Road to the Presidency: Women of Color Assuming Leadership Roles in the Academy

African-American Female College Presidents' Career Paths

Anna L. Waring

Abstract

To date, little research has been done on the circumstances that have brought African-American women to the presidency of colleges and universities. In fall 1997, there were 46 African-American women serving as college and university presidents. The majority (55%) headed junior and community colleges. The rest were at satellite state university campuses or Historically Black Colleges and Universities (HBCUs). Only one president served at a prestigious institution and she headed a traditionally women's college. Most of the discussion about diversity at colleges and universities in this country has been directed toward the diversification of the undergraduate student body, not the executive levels of administration. We must better understand the mobility patterns of women of color in colleges and universities and how their presence shapes the image of the institutions they lead. This research addresses these questions: (1) What has been the career path of African-American women to the college presidency? Do these career paths differ from the career paths of other college presidents?, and (2) What are the personal backgrounds of these presidents and how have their backgrounds influenced their career achievements and aspirations?

Introduction

In order to understand how African-American women ascended to the college presidency, it is important to locate their experiences in larger bodies of empirical and theoretical research. The research that has informed this study is drawn from the work on: career paths in higher education; the role of gender in higher education career paths; and the interaction of race and gender in understanding the experiences of women of color.

Career Paths in Higher Education

There are career ladders in higher education as there are in other professions. Once a person begins in one career ladder, say in community colleges, it is difficult to transfer to another career ladder. So, the first job after a degree is very important in determining the potential career trajectory for each individual. Wessel and Keim (1994) found that in private four-year institutions, there are two primary routes to the presidency - academic or administrative. The majority of presidents (69%) came through the academic career path. The percentage of presidents going through the academic path is higher for presidents at doctoral granting institutions (83%) than at liberal arts colleges (69%) and comprehensive (66%) institutions. This study indicates that faculty experience is a necessary precursor for the presidency at higher status institutions, the findings are less clear for presidents at other types of institutions.

The majority of college presidents (58.4%) had Ph.D. degrees, followed by the Ed.D. at 22.2%. Ten percent of the presidents held a masters degree, these most likely were presidents of the for-profit institutions (The Chronicle of Higher Education Almanac, 1999). The type of credentials a president has influences the type of institutions he is likely to head.

During the 1998-1999 academic year, the median tenure for college presidents was six years. The assumption is that the typical route to the presidency is through the academic path and this is still largely true. Seventy-three percent of the presidents had been faculty members, though slightly less than a quarter (22.8%) had been faculty members for only one to five years. The median was six years as a faculty member, an indication that presidents decided, or were tapped early on, for careers in administration.

Gender and Higher Education

Gender stratification is a stable feature in colleges and universities. Women hold different jobs than do their male counterparts. On average, male faculty receive tenure in less time, earn more money, leave faculty positions less often and have been faculty members longer than have female faculty (McElrath 1992). In addition, women are more likely to be administrators in community colleges than in four-year institutions (Warner 1988).

Women tend to occupy staff positions that are marginal to the mission of the institution (counseling, positions for women, and positions for other minorities), though their educational background is not significantly different from men. The fact that women are in different positions results in cumulative disadvantage for them (Johnsrud and Heck 1994). Women administrators in higher education tended to report perceptions of more barriers to upward mobility in higher education than did men. The barriers that women cited were lack of strong sponsorship for administrative positions, sex discrimination, family responsibilities and their education (Warner 1988).

The Interaction of Race and Gender

There is little literature exploring how race and gender interact in establishing career paths for women of color in higher education. Most of the demographic statistics on administrators in higher education provide information on race and on gender, but they do not address the interaction effect of race and gender. Recent studies have begun to indicate the importance of looking at this interaction so as to understand the experiences of women of color as they may or may not be distinct from the experiences of men of color and majority women. For example, a recent analysis of baccalaureate degrees of successful women found important differences among African-American, Latina, and Caucasian women that had been obscured when the women were treated as a monolithic group (Wolf-Wendel 1998). This research and other research by Bell, Denton and Nkomo (1993) suggest that it is important to understand the role race plays when looking at differences among females.

In the last decade there have been five published dissertations on African-American female presidents. The importance of the role of race in these studies is mixed. African-American female presidents tend to parallel their Caucasian counterparts with respect to age when they assumed the presidency and length of tenure in office (Sanford-Harris 1990; Kane 1997). Arnold (1994) reports that African-American female presidents felt that being black and female had worked in their favor. Sanford-Harris (1990) found that race was more salient as the women reported that the discrimination they had faced dealt more with race than gender. Finally, Kane (1997) found no appreciable differences in the career paths of Caucasian and African-American female college presidents. Even with these dissertations, there is a need for a comprehensive study of these women to address how they come to the college presidency and how they perform once they are presidents.

Methodology

To understand career paths of African-American female college presidents it was important to document the types of jobs these women had, how these jobs may have led them to become college presidents, and how their career paths were similar to or different from majority-male presidents. In order to explore these areas, I interviewed the presidents and reviewed their curriculum vitae. In the interviews, I asked about career intentions at important transition points such as first job after college, first job in a higher education institution, and jobs immediately prior to assuming their first presidency.

I interviewed twelve African-American female college presidents for one to two hours each. Six of the respondents were presidents at community colleges and six were presidents at four-year institutions. Of the presidents at four-year institutions, five were presidents of state or publicly institutions and one was a president of a private institution (See TABLE 1 for a list of institutions).

Ten of the interviews were face-to-face while two were telephone interviews. Leland and Astin (1991) developed a questionnaire that they used for a research project on women administrators in colleges and universities. I used this questionnaire as the primary guide for this research. The part of the interview protocol that focused on career paths asked questions about the presidents' educational background, the career history, reasons for entering and changing careers, and their family backgrounds.

Findings

Johnsrud and Heck (1994) argue that gender stratification is a stable feature in colleges and universities. There appear to be dominant characteristics that determine the differences in career trajectory for men and women in colleges and universities - terminal degree type and type of jobs one holds. Women, more than men, tend to opt for degrees in education and take jobs in the support side of the university. These decisions, in general, hold true for the 12 African-American female college presidents whom I interviewed in this study.

Advanced Degrees

Advanced degree type is important for understanding administrators' career advancement in colleges and universities. Warner (1988) found two factors important to career advancement to higher level administrative positions - one's education and one's faculty experience. In Warner's study, a majority of women held their advanced degree in education while men held degrees from a variety of fields and disciplines. These women tended to hold lower level positions than did the men and were more likely to be administrators in community colleges.

In my research, only two of the twelve presidents did not have advanced degrees in Education. One of the presidents had a J.D. degree and another had a Ph.D. in Psychobiology. The general consensus from the presidents was that they were or became committed to working in higher education and they thought that an advanced degree in Education was the best way to gain entry into the administrative side of the university.

Four of the twelve presidents had education degrees at the undergraduate level. The others majored in academic disciplines such as psychology, history, and sociology, though two did have undergraduate degrees in nursing. However, the variation in degree type at the undergraduate level begins to disappear at the master's degree level where all but five received masters degrees in education related fields. Those who did not receive master's degrees in education received their degrees in psychology (2), social work, and communications.

Types of Jobs

The funneling of the presidents into educational master's and doctoral programs is associated with the types of jobs they took immediately after college. Not surprisingly for African-American women graduating from college in the 1960s, all but one chose careers in the helping professions of education, counseling, and nursing. The one respondent who chose another career path went directly from college to a doctoral program in Psychobiology; after gaining her Ph.D. she worked as a researcher for more than a decade before changing careers. Seven worked as teachers - four in high school, two in junior high school, and one in elementary school. Two were practicing nurses, one was an assistant professor of Psychology, and one was a coordinator of an academic support center at a college.

Entry into Community Colleges

The six women who were presidents of community colleges reported that community colleges were more receptive to them than other types of educational institutions. Also, they report that community colleges tended to work with the type of students (minority, underprepared, vocationally-oriented, etc.) that they were committed to seeing become successful.

The four presidents who were high school teachers were recruited in community colleges. At that time, high school teaching experience and master's level graduate work were sufficient for being a faculty member in community colleges. One of the respondents stated that she would have preferred to continue working in public schools, however, it was easier to get a job in a community college than in her local public school district. Of the other community college presidents, one who had majored in nursing began teaching in a four-year private institution but when she relocated to another city, it too was easier to teach in a community college than in another type of institution. This respondent was pursuing a doctorate in psychology when she had to return home to care for an ailing parent. Again, the local community college was the one place that would hire her with a master's degree.

While the presidents at the community colleges reported that they were drawn to community colleges because of the type of students community colleges serve, only one was a president of a college educating primarily African-American students. Four of the presidents headed institutions that were majority Caucasian and one headed a college that was approximately half and half Caucasian and Native American. One of these presidents headed the second largest community college in the United States and another one of these presidents headed one of the most prestigious because of its membership in the League for Innovation, which works with 25 select community colleges on technology and curricular reform. Four of the six presidents were holding their second or third presidency, each having come from a smaller community college.

Entry into Four-Year Institutions

Presidents of four-year institutions, while having had similar work and educational backgrounds to community college presidents, were either recruited into four-year institutions or saw four-year institutions as a way that they could help students become successful.

Two of the six presidents were recruited into higher education by their dissertation advisors. One of the two reported that she wanted a doctorate so that she could eventually become a superintendent of public schools; however, her advisor told her that he would not work with her unless she was planning to become a professor. The other president recruited into the faculty profession also had a dissertation advisor who opened doors for her and advocated for her in job searches.

Two of the presidents came into higher education, on the administrative side, from other professions. One was recruited in because of her financial experience a nd o ne sought a p osition a fter t iring of a n onacademic job. The final two presidents came to four-year institutions because they wanted to better serve Black students. One of the two held a variety of academic support positions in f our-year institutions while the other one entered higher education at the presidential level after a career in research and politics.

The community college presidents were more likely to head institutions with small African-American populations, whereas, four of the six presidents at four-year institutions headed institutions that served almost exclusively African-American students. Of the two presidents who headed institutions with mostly Caucasian student bodies, one had been a long-time employee of the university and the other followed a more traditional career path to the presidency than did others in the study.

Routes to the Presidency

For the presidents of community colleges, nearly all gained some teaching experience in post-secondary institutions through their work in community colleges. Only one became president of a community college without some teaching experience and she came from administrative experience in the central office of a multi-campus community college system.

While these community college presidents had some teaching experience, none of them stayed teachers long. They were identified and groomed by deans and presidents who encouraged them to gather skills that would serve them as they climbed the administrative ladder. All of the respondents said that their mentors told them that they would need advanced degrees instead of a Ph.D. or Ed. D. in Education. In addition, five of the six community college presidents were active members of professional associations and shared advice and support with other African-American community college presidents and those interested in becoming presidents.

Interestingly, in the case of presidents of four-year institutions, only one followed a traditional academic career path - first being a faculty member, then a dean, then a provost, and then a campus head. The other presidents came through administrative positions or were recruited to the presidency from a nonprofit educational organization. These non-traditional career paths may explain why African-American women tend to head lower status colleges and universities.

The Role of Mentors

All the presidents indicated that mentors played an important role in their development. The mentors were both professional and personal.

Professional Mentors

Ten of the twelve presidents indicated that they took on or were given increasingly difficult and/or higher profile jobs that got them noticed. Each built a track record of success that brought them to the attention of senior administrators in their institutions. Of the two who did not indicate that they had some form of professional mentoring, one had come from outside of higher education into the presidency and one had her name submitted to a community college presidential search while serving as a faculty member at a four-year institution.

Of the twelve respondents, four indicated that presidents, usually at their institutions, indicated that they should begin preparing themselves for a presidency. Three of the four women who reported having a president tap them were in community colleges. One president-mentor created an unofficial internship to allow this community college president to gain exposure to the various duties and tasks of the president. She attended senior staff and board meetings for more than a year and after that the president-mentor began recommending her for searches. In the case of another community college president, her chancellor submitted her name for the presidency of the largest community college in the district. While she was turned down for that presidency, she was selected as president of the smallest college in the district and a few years later became president of the two institutions when they were merged. The sole president in a private four-year institution reported that presidents at Historically Black Colleges and Universities approved of the work she did with their association and suggested that she should consider a presidency.

Personal Mentors

In addition to professional mentors, all the presidents reported having a variety of personal mentors. All cite the role of their parents or guardian's as critical factors in their development. Regardless of whether their parents were educated beyond high school or not, all indicated that their parents or guardians encouraged them educationally. One president was an orphan and credits the local nuns with instilling in her a love of learning and a belief in her possibilities.

In a ddition t o s upporting t heir e ducational a spirations, many p arents also provided useful advice about how to "read" people and interact with others. Two specifically cited their mothers as mentors in helping them learn how to develop an intuitive sense of people. Some of this sense of how to read people, and the need to do so, came from being raised in the South during segregation.

Conclusions and Recommendations

The twelve presidents who participated in this study were atypical with respect to the larger population of college and university presidents. Besides the obvious differences of race and gender, these women differed in advanced degree type and career paths to the presidency from the typical Caucasian male college or university president. A lthough, they did share similar characteristics of other female administrators in higher education.

All but two of these women had an advanced degree in education or educational administration, compared to about a quarter of all presidents. Because of the strong effect that degree type can have on entry into type of post-secondary education, this appears to be an important factor in the large number of African American women who head community colleges and lower-status four-year institutions. Part of the reason for the over-representation of educational degrees is that these women entered into careers that were available to them - primarily teaching. Once in the field of education, they opted for degrees that they thought would best prepare them for upward mobility. While about a quarter of all college and university presidents do have advanced degrees in education, few of the presidents with this type of degree head the more prestigious institutions.

These women's career paths to the presidency were also different from the majority of the other college and university presidents. These women report a strong commitment to working with students who have a hard time gaining access to post-secondary education. Since working with these students was a dominant motivation, many of these women opted for administrative positions on the support side of the university. It was from these administrative support positions that most of the women moved up in administration, unlike the majority of male presidents who spent some time in the faculty. Again, these non-traditional career paths could explain why so few African-American women head higher status colleges and universities.

While there was a large degree of choice among these women to work with non-traditional students, it is difficult to know whether they chose education degrees and administrative support positions or whether these were the only positions available to them. In two cases, having a dissertation advisor play an active role set them on a career path that took them to faculty positions in four-year institutions. We need to understand better the role that the dissertation advisor plays in launching women of color into careers in higher education.

While community colleges are perceived to be lower status institutions, African-American women have had slightly more success in achieving the presidency in these institutions than in four-year colleges and universities. In addition, African-American women presidents seem to head a wider variety of community colleges than is true in the four-year institutions. It is possible that the expectation that people of color should head institutions with large minority populations is more firmly entrenched in four-year institutions than is the case in community colleges. Future research needs to explore the barriers that exist at four-year institutions that keep them from facilitating the upward mobility of females in general, and African-American women in particular.

In light of findings from this and other research, there are a number of recommendations for African-American females who might be interested in becoming college or university presidents.

1. Consider a doctoral degree in an academic discipline instead of education. The typical college or university president, especially at elite and research universities, tend to have academic doctorates.

2. Try to choose a dissertation advisor who will be an advocate for you as you go on the job market. Your advisor should be willing to use his or her professional contacts on your behalf.

3. Once you have your doctoral degree, be very careful about your first job. Career ladders in higher education make it difficult to move between two-and four-year institutions. Though two of the community college presidents had experience in four-year institutions, one reported that

it took her a very long time to convince people in community colleges that she really wanted to work in those types of institutions.

4. Spend some time as a faculty member. While the amount of time presidents spent as faculty members is declining, most presidents were faculty members before becoming presidents.

5. When possible, get a mentor who will give you advice, but more importantly will recommend you in the job search process. Successful presidents have strong advocates who keep them informed of opportunities and advise them about their careers.

6. Develop a professional reputation as a hard and good worker and people will volunteer to be your mentor. About half the respondents in this research indicated that people liked their work ethic and offered to help them with their careers.

7. Think about the best way to be an advocate for African-American and other minority students. Administrative positions may provide more direct support to students; however, these positions may stall one's upward mobility in colleges and universities.

8. Develop alliances with other women and people of color to keep informed about professional opportunities and as ways to support one another. The presidents at community colleges have a much better developed network of contacts than do the presidents at four-year institutions. This network seems to be one factor in the increasing numbers of African-American female college presidents in these institutions.

References

American Council on Education. *Mailing list of African-American female presidents.* 1997.

Arnold, Shirley. "A Descriptive Study of the Characteristics of Black Women College Presidents/Chief Executive Officers." (Ph.D. diss., Georgia State University, 1994).

Astin, Helen S. and Carole Leland. *Women of Influence, Women of Vision.* San Francisco: Jossey-Bass Publishers, 1991.

Bell, Ella L., Toni C. Denton and Stella Nkomo. "Women of Color in Management: Toward an Inclusive Analysis in Women Managers: Trends, Issues, and Challenges in Managerial Diversity." Vol. 4. *Women and Work.* Newbury Park, CA: Sage Publications, 1993.

Bell, Ella L. and Stella Nkomo. "Re-visioning Women Manager's Lives" in *Gendering Organizational Analysis,* edited by Albert J. Mills and Peta Tancred. Newbury Park: Sage Publications, 1992.

Chase, Pearline. "Black Women College Presidents: Perceptions of their Major Job Roles, Problems, Expectations, and Experiences." (Ph.D. diss., Harvard University, 1987).

Giddings, Paula. *When and Where I Enter: The Impact of Black Women on Race and Sex in America.* New York: William Morrow, 1984.

Green, Madeline F. *The American College President: A Contemporary Profile.* Washington, DC: American Council on Education.

Helgesen, Sally. *The Female Advantage: Women's Ways of Leadership.* New York: Doubleday, 1990.

Hill-Collins, Patricia. *Black Feminist Thought: Knowledge, Consciousness and the Politics of Empowerment.* 2nd ed. New York: Routledge (sp), 2000.

Johnsrud, Linda K. and Ronald H. Heck. "Administrative Promotion within a University: The Cumulative Impact of Gender." *The Journal of Higher Education.* January/February (1994): 23-44.

Kane, Jacqueline. "Differences in the Career Lines of Black and White Women College Presidents." (Ph.D. diss., State University of New York at Albany, 1997).

McElrath, Karen. "Gender, Career Disruption, and Academic Rewards." *The Journal of Higher Education.* May/June (1992): 267-281.

Moses, Yolanda. *Black Women in Academe: Issues and Strategies.* Washington, D.C.: Association of American Colleges and Universities.

Robinson, Florine Cato. "Preparing African-American Women for the Community College Presidency: Implications for Adult Continuing Education." Ph.D. diss., Northern Illinois University, 1996.

Sanford-Harris, Judith L. "A Profile of Black Women College Presidents and Chief Executive Officers. (Ph.D. diss., Boston

College, 1990).

Wessel, Roger D. and Marybell C. Kiem. "Career Patterns of Private Four-Year College and University Presidents in the United States." *The Journal of Higher Education*. March/April (1994): 211-225.

Wolfman, Brunetta Reid. "Light as from a Beacon: African American Women Administrators in the Academy," in *Black Women in the Academy: Promises and Perils*. Gainesville, FL: University of Florida Press, (1997): 158-167.

Wolf-Wendel, Lisa E. "Models of Excellence: The Baccalaureate Origins of Successful European American Women, African American Women and Latinas." *The Journal of Higher Education*. March/April (1998): 141-186.

The Road Less Traveled

Dolores M. Fernández
**President, Eugenio María de Hostos Community
College of The City University of New York**

There are many textbook theories about how administrators arrive at the positions they hold. Some may have had well-thought-out plans based on theoretical designs that provided a roadmap to their destination. However, I am not one of those administrators, so if you are looking for such a map, I suggest that you look elsewhere, because this reflection will take you down "the road less traveled and filled with many land mines."

My road to the presidency has been very non-traditional, if there is such a thing. I went from being a full professor with tenure at one college of The City University of New York on a Friday afternoon to being the "interim college president" of another CUNY institution on the following Monday morning.

Assuming a leadership position under the tenuous conditions that existed when I stepped into the president's office at Eugenio María de Hostos Community College was a professional challenge greater than anything I could have imagined; and yet I took it. Fortunately, administrative experience was something that I had to offer. Equally important was the fact that I had the resiliency that comes from being a Hispanic and a woman. This resiliency served me well long before I became a college president, and it continues to do so.

Originally I went into education to be a teacher, but even then my route did not take me along a traditional path. While I had always dreamed of teaching, I entered the profession belatedly because my dream was temporarily derailed. As a result of this derailment, one thing I have shared with young people along the different paths I have traveled is that there are no expiration dates on dreams.

At the age of fifteen, I lost my father, with whom I shared a special bond. He was a true role model and I loved him very much. His illness and death devastated me even more than I realized at the time. I took the PSAT during his last months, even though I was not in the right state of mind to perform well at that time. As a result, I scored abysmally on the examination, and then my dad passed away two months later. This happened in July during what I consider the lost summer of my life. In September of that year, I was called into the counselor's office at my high school to be told that in view of my very poor performance on the PSAT, I needed to reconsider my career goals, as I was not college material. While this may have been a natural reaction to a student who had performed poorly on a standardized examination, in my case there were definitely extenuating circumstances. I was a member of Arista, the national honor society; my high school GPA was above 3.5; and when I eventually graduated from college, I ranked tenth in a class of 600. How can one account for this rush to judgment by a professional who should have known better? Did he cast me in a stereotypical role that he reserved for all Latinas? Whatever this counselor's reason may have been, I was naive enough to accept his verdict. Consequently, instead of attending college immediately after high school, I enrolled in a secretarial program that provided me with the skills I needed to enter the business world.

However, my dream of teaching never died; it was only deferred. As time passed, a nagging voice inside me kept repeating, "You can do it; just go for it." Ten years later, at the age of 26 with two young children in tow, I stepped onto the campus of Nassau Community College and enrolled as a freshman. This marked the beginning of a seventeen-year journey that culminated on a spring afternoon in 1988 when I walked across the stage at Hofstra University to receive my doctoral degree. From the audience, I could hear cheers of "Bravo, Dr. Mom!" from my three children, and as one journey ended, another began.

I learned many things during the journey to my doctorate. Some of the lessons came from academic learning, but others involved learning who I was, where I had come from, and where I was going. At times, the rites of passage were painful, but the experiences they provided were always worthwhile. I learned to have confidence in myself, and in the process, I found that I missed my father even more, because I would never be able to share with him all that I had accomplished since he left my side. In the course of my journey, I also learned to recognize when I was being judged on the basis of my ethnicity, language, and culture. That learning process also taught me how to deal with biased individuals by showing them that I was just as capable as my colleagues.

Paradoxically, the low expectations that many in this society have for minority group members can work to our advantage if we strive to achieve 150% when others get by with 90% or less. By giving our all, we are able to outshine and outperform the competition, and leave them in the dust. I've shared this lesson with my children and with the innumerable minority students I have encountered in the course of my career.

Because I was motivated to produce more than what was expected of me at the beginning of my teaching career, I was offered the opportunity to "teach teachers," which sounded like an interesting and challenging undertaking. I did not seek this opportunity; rather, administrators identified me as someone who had the potential for sharing what she did best with other members of her profession. The teacher trainer position I was offered also had a quasi-administrative aspect, in that it involved providing service to school districts in Nassau and Suffolk counties in New York State. A major responsibility was working with school superintendents and deputy superintendents for curriculum and instruction in those districts. This was a valuable learning experience for me in that I truly became aware of the many roles that district-level administrators must play in order to maintain a school system of the highest (or even not so high) quality. This position opened doors of opportunity and helped me advance to the next challenging role in my career.

When an opening occurred for a Director of Education in a New York State agency that was responsible for juvenile delinquents and offenders, I applied. Although I thought that my chance of being hired for this position was probably remote, I responded when I was called for an interview, chalking it up to a learning opportunity in which I would find out what was expected of someone applying for a job at that level. After a lengthy process, I was offered the position. Although this took me by surprise, I accepted the offer and made the necessary arrangements to relocate my family to upstate New York. I learned many things as Director of Education for the New York State Division for Youth. Initially, the people who were to report to me thought I was "just another political appointee" and would probably be very limited in what I knew and what I could bring to the position. Once again, I was being judged on the basis of a stereotype. Nevertheless, in a very brief period, I gained the respect of my staff. It didn't take them long to discover that their snap judgment of this Latina had been entirely wrong. While the staff was learning about me, I was learning about the young people who had been sent to these residential facilities by the New York judicial system. I came to realize that all young people want to learn, regardless of their physical setting or circumstances in life. The population of students for which this agency was responsible presented many challenges, and I am pleased to say that I managed to meet these challenges and overcome most of them.

In my work with the Division for Youth, it became apparent to me that regardless of whether the classroom is in a public school in New York City or in a residential facility upstate, education is education. In order for young people to learn, their teacher must care for them and listen to them. As an administrator, you discover very quickly that you must determine the scope of your responsibility. When I accepted this position, I knew very little about the juvenile justice system. Therefore, I made a point of visiting every such facility in the state during my first year on the job. This gave me the opportunity to meet many youngsters who had been written off by society and the traditional education system. Even so, through the efforts of the committed and caring staff employed at these sites, they were making progress academically.

After four years, another opportunity for professional advancement came my way. I submitted my name and curriculum vitae for a position that was advertised in a highly regarded newspaper in the field of education. A Deputy Chancellor for Curriculum and Instruction was being sought by New York City Public Schools. Again I applied not really expecting to be interviewed, but to my surprise, the Chancellor's Office called to schedule an appointment with me.

If you were to ask my children, "Which of the positions that your mother held had the greatest impact on your lives?" all three would answer, "Deputy Chancellor." This job was all consuming, 24/7, and at times it seemed as to demand even more. However, it proved to be almost as brief as it was demanding. When the Chancellor who hired me passed away a year after I had joined his administrative team, I decided not to continue with the subsequent administration. By the time I left, I had been in this position for less than two years; but because the experience was so intense, it seemed considerably longer. From an administrative perspective, I believe it prepared me for whatever job I might hold in the future. Not only did I gain invaluable insight into the politics of education, I also developed the skills to negotiate with unions, superintendents, school personnel, and parents. As hard as the work had been, I found it very gratifying. However, emotional occurrences during those years took their toll. Working for Chancellor Richard Green, I learned to respect professionals who are hired for specific roles and hold them accountable for fulfilling the responsibilities of their positions. Dr. Green serves as a shining example of what it means to be a very humanistic administrator, and the lessons I learned from him will remain with me always.

Upon leaving the New York City Board of Education, I accepted a position as a professor at Hunter College of The City University of New York. While I welcomed the opportunity to return to teaching at the college level, I found that once administration gets under your skin, you tend to gravitate toward administrative responsibilities at different levels. At Hunter, I soon became involved in designing and administering programs that prepared teachers to work in the most troubled schools and districts in New York City.

My primary administrative assignment was to coordinate the Administration and Supervision Program, a post-graduate certificate-bearing course of study for aspiring principals and/or superintendents. I also served as co-coordinator of a collaborative project with Brown University, so while I was teaching, a multitude of other responsibilities enabled me to cultivate the administrative skills and maintain the connections that I had developed with professionals in New York City public schools.

After I had been at Hunter for several years, circumstances arose that led to a change of administration at a community college within the City University system. The institution in transition was Eugenio María de Hostos Community College, and in March of 1998 I was appointed as the Interim President and given the charge of implementing a process of institutional regeneration within a two-year timeframe.

As I was unfamiliar with Hostos, I began by visiting every department and meeting with the faculty, staff, and students to share my vision for the institution, which was (and is) "to make Eugenio María de Hostos Community College a college of excellence for students seeking a liberal arts or career education in a multilingual/multicultural learning environment." At one of these meetings, a faculty member remarked that what I was proposing sounded like a "renaissance," and thus the Hostos Renaissance began.

HOSTOS RENAISSANCE—1998-2000
To everything is a season, and a time to every purpose...
a time to break down, and a time to build up....
--Ecclesiastes 3:1, 3

On March 2, 2003, I began my fifth year as President of Hostos Community College. My experiences here have been both enriching and trying, and I have learned from every one of them. One of the most important things I learned was that the opportunity should never be taken away from the faculty and staff of an institution of higher education to have a say in the selection of their president. The faculty and staff of Hostos were denied this opportunity when, after I had served on an interim basis for a year, the Board of Trustees appointed me as President of the school.

Soon thereafter, I learned another important thing. Even though I came to this position with expertise in language acquisition and in designing dual language instructional programs, this was not my role at Hostos. My role was to be the president, not the provost. Next I had a refresher course in negotiating with unions in order to reach the goals that would move this institution forward. I also learned the importance of keeping all constituent groups on campus informed about what is happening. This is essential for obtaining a total buy-in at the outset of any initiative. Moreover, the students are one of the most important constituent groups in any school. All of these lessons were learned under battle conditions because this college and the CUNY system had been the object of a very negative media campaign that had been going on for quite some time. As a result of relentlessly bad press, it was very difficult to recruit a permanent administrative team. Highly qualified candidates simply did not apply for positions at Hostos. Therefore, for the first three years of my tenure, my administrative team consisted of acting vice presidents and acting deans.

To complicate matters further, the school was due for a Middle States reaccreditation visit during this period, and at the same time, the need to redesign two major academic areas became apparent. This involved relieving the English Department of its responsibility for instruction in English as a second language, thereby enhancing its offerings in traditional English courses on writing and literature. All English as a second language components were reassigned to a new department that was named Language and Cognition. This major change was met with some resistance, and a degree of dissention is still present within the faculty. However, the division of labor was part of a concerted effort to work with the Professional Staff Congress, the union representing faculty members in the CUNY system. I consider it a major accomplishment of the past year and a half that no one on my administrative team has "acting" in front of his or her title. While appointed vice presidents are assisting me in setting the course for the college's future, they are extending a trail that was blazed by their predecessors who served in an acting capacity. The hard work and dedication of these administrators past and present has transformed this institution to such an extent that my vision of Hostos as a college of excellence is most assuredly becoming a reality.

This progress is all the more significant, considering that the majority of the faculty and staff have been here since the college was established and have seen administrations come and go with the political winds that are forever changing. Surviving a series of caretaker administrations contributed to the apathy of some long-term personnel, who developed an attitude of "Let's wait and see; maybe they'll go away." Now that a "permanent" administrative team is in place, the faculty, staff, and students have realized that positive change is possible, and they welcome the opportunity to be part of the mechanism that will bring it about.

In the past year and a half, a core curriculum was approved and will be implemented in the fall semester of 2003. The mission statement of the college has also been reconsidered, reworded, and ratified by the faculty, staff, and students. The revised version clarifies and reaffirms our commitment to the community this institution was established to serve. Efforts to recruit students in local high schools are proving very successful, with the result that we are now enrolling a younger student population that is diversifying the culture of the school. In response to their needs, Hostos has established athletic teams that have elevated school spirit to a record high. New learning labs are now in place, and the library that was once an embarrassment is now considered "state of the art." The revitalization of Hostos Community College is by no means finished, but we have turned a significant corner and come a considerable distance along the pathway to excellence. As a result, there is new hope within the institution and new confidence in the community that our vision can be achieved. There is also a clear understanding that we must press on until we reach a state of excellence, and once there, we must never turn back. Administrators need a sixth sense that tells them when it is time to leave an institution. As of now, my sixth sense is telling me that this time has not yet come. I do not feel that my presidency, which is to say my work at Hostos has been completed. Much has been accomplished, but there is still much more to be done, and I am very proud to be doing it.

From Sorrow Valley to the Presidency

Algeania Warren Freeman
President, Livingstone College & Hood Theological Seminary

Perhaps, I have been on this leadership journey all of my life. For from my earliest memories, I have always wanted to lead. Whether playing with paper dolls, jump rope, or hopscotch, there was always a passion or a yearning within me to direct the traffic. It was at my college graduation in May 1970 that I realized I wanted to earn a doctorate degree and spend the remainder of my life working and making a difference as an administrator in the academy. Though I had the dream within, the road towards fulfilling the dream was not easy. Yet, persistence with a strong determination not to allow my dream to be deferred kept me focused on the promise land.

Born in a community called Sorrow Valley in a small rural town next to the trash dump made me realize that God must have something significant for me to do with my future. Picking cotton, barning tobacco, and picking up sweet potatoes in hot fields with the sun sweltering on my back left a blazing determination within me to get an education.

Sorrow Valley was a unique place, because it was the area in town designated for African Americans. It always puzzled me why a community would be named Sorrow Valley. Did it mean that people who lived there were destined for tremendous trials and tribulations? Did it mean that the neighborhood residents were disposable commodities? Whatever the meaning of Sorrow Valley, it propelled me to seek a greater destiny. Sorrow Valley made me more determined to fulfill the leadership anointing that I believed God had placed in my genetic make-up before sending me to planet earth.

As shared, from my earliest memories, I have always been involved in leadership activities whether in church, in the Girl Scouts, or 4-H Clubs. Even in college, I served as the president of the Pan-Hellenic Council. In this student leadership position, I had the opportunity to work very closely with the University's Chancellor. From that association, I was smitten with the desire to become an administrator in higher education. The chancellor has continued to serve as a lifelong mentor and career coach for me.

As soon as I earned a doctorate degree, I accepted a leadership position as a department chair at a historically black college/university (HBCU). My commitment to work at an HBCU stemmed from the excellent educational experience that I had during my undergraduate studies at an HBCU. The early position as a department chair taught me many leadership lessons. The day before I started the position, an older woman administrator sat me down, and she taught me how to develop an agenda that would allow me to accomplish desired outcomes while keeping the meetings on target. It was during this time that I became a serious student studying the inner workings of the academy. Chairing a multifaceted department with six academic programs allowed me to gain a cross discipline perspective. I learned about accreditation requirements for the academic programs that I supervised. I also gained tremendous experience in learning how to finesse a nd w ork with difficult or eccentric people.

Trying to keep my career on track has been a difficult task, because I wanted to be a wife and mother. I married a career man whose profession as an urban planner and my desire to have a career caused us to move 17 times during our 31 years of marriage. Three times, we had a commuter marriage with some commutes having six-hour separations. During one commuter marriage, I had the task of rearing a six-year old son who was traumatized by the move and by having to leave the place of his birth and his friends. In spite of all the personal family sacrifices, my husband and I arrived at the pinnacle of our careers almost at the same time. Our son also thrived; although during one move, I had to commute 180 miles every day in some of the worse traffic America has to offer so that I could ensure that our son would have the educational and emotional support that he needed for success in life. This year, our son is completing his undergraduate degree at Stanford University with honors as a PAC-10 Academic All American Football Player.

On the road to the presidency, there are several things which I believed help to shape my career as well as prepare me for my current position. **The career experiences were:**

- H eld positions as a department chair and dean where I administered multi-faceted academic units. Most of these units had between six to twenty academic programs. Most of the programs had accreditation standards that had to be satisfied. As an administrator, I had the opportunity to learn about and work with professionals across disciplines in order to satisfy the professional requirements of the disciplines. Preparing self-study reports for accreditation allowed me to develop my writing skills.

- In the various administrative positions, I had to administer large as well as many complex budgets. I attended workshops and seminars every chance that I got to learn how to prepare and manage fiscal budgets.

- In order to manage multi-faceted academic units, strategic planning became a critical element. Again, I attended workshops and seminars so that I could learn how to build consensus, develop and implement strategic plans and strategic direction documents. I also learned that it was extremely critical to have a strategic evaluation component. These components led me to personalize this process so that not only did we have plans for the academic units, but during the academic year, the faculty also had faculty activity plans (FAP), faculty activity reports (FAR), and faculty activity evaluations (FAE).

- I held one position as the assistant vice president for academic planning and program development. This position allowed me to plan and work collaboratively with others to implement new degree programs.

- A lesson learned early was that a critical key to success as an administrator in the academy is to be well organized. I learned to never attend a meeting with out a written agenda. I also learned to complete and submit required work assignments such as plans and reports before the date(s) requested.

- To strengthen both my oral and written communication skills, I practiced often. I also involved myself in activities where I would have speaking and writing opportunities.

▪ Whenever asked, I took advantage of the opportunity to represent my president or vice president at local, regional and national meetings. While attending the meetings, I made a special effort to network and to meet people.

▪ While serving as a department chair, I realized that I wanted to become a president at a college or university. I looked for development opportunities that would help me to strengthen my leadership skills. It was during my tenure as a department chair that I personally paid for and attended a professional development seminar on the preparation and nuances of becoming a college president. This was one of the best workshops that I ever attended. In the seminar, I learned how to develop an eye-catching resume, how to handle interview questions, and even how to dress for the interview. Along the way, I made sure that in each position as a dean, vice president, and president that I attended leadership seminars such as the Management Development Program, Management for Lifelong Learning, and New Presidents' Institute at Harvard University. I also had a strong desire to have someone else assess or critique my leadership skills so that I could improve in the areas that needed to be enhanced. I attended the Looking Glass Leadership Program. The most impressive component of the program was learning about how others viewed my leadership skills and potential ability as a leader. A priority for me was to read as many books on leadership and study as many leaders as I could. What I wanted was to glean knowledge about successes and failures of leaders.

▪ Learning how to obtain external fiscal support for programs was essential for my leadership advancement. I took workshops on the art of writing grant proposals. I also attended a weeklong program at Dartmouth on the art of fund raising. It is extremely important to learn how to identify potential donors, cultivate donors, and to ultimately make the "**ask**" for funds and resource support. I also wrote many grant proposals. As a department chair, several major grants were funded that demonstrated to others that I could obtain external funding support if selected for higher leadership positions.

▪ Wherever I worked, I always tried to develop at least one creative centerpiece program. At one institution, a hazardous waste management institute was established with funding support from the environmental protection agency. At another institution, an academic village program was established with a goal of providing students with a holistic preparation during their matriculation. Demonstrating that you are creative can be the difference in being selected or not selected for a senior-level position.

▪ Being mobile also allowed me to obtain a wealth of experience. To advance, several times, I had to assume positions where I was the first African American administrator. I also wanted to participate in diverse cultural work experiences so that when selected for a senior-level position, I would have different views and perspectives on how to administer an institution.

▪ Networking is critical. I have nurtured and maintained professional friendships for years. Whenever I have needed a written or oral reference, my network of professional colleagues always gave me the inside "scoop" about a job I was interested in pursuing. They also gave me positive references during the search process. It is absolutely critical that one selects individuals they can trust to provide positive references. These references can make or break your career aspirations.

▪ I t is also important to attend professional meetings as well as to look for other unique experiences that will give one a wide breadth of leadership moments. It is great if one can assume leadership positions within a professional association. I served as the president of the National Allied Health Association and the executive director of the National Black Association for Speech, Language and Hearing. I also was honored with my selection as a fellow of the American Allied Health Association. I served as a consultant in allied health twice in South Africa for the W.K. Kellogg Foundation so that I could gain international experience. It was an extremely significant leadership opportunity when I was selected to serve on a congressionally mandated National Academy of Sciences/Institute of Medicine study committee on allied health. It was on this committee where I had the opportunity to meet and work with the former president of Johns Hopkins University and the current president of the W.K. Kellogg foundation. This association has been nurtured and maintained through all stages of my career from serving as a dean to becoming a president.

▪ I t is important to look for special programs that will development your leadership position as well as propel you ahead. For example, I applied for and became a national finalist for the white house fellows program. Although I was not selected as a fellow, the interview experience and background check provided invaluable experience for my development as a leader.

▪ H aving persevered during 30 years as an administrator and professor in the academy, I have learned m any precious l essons. Some of the experiences were heart breaking and heart wrenching. However, I learned "to take the bitter with the sweet." For there is truth in the adage "no burning; no learning". It took me years to learn that I needed all the wonderful experiences along with the awful experiences for my making, growth, and development.

▪ O ut of these experiences, I have developed a philosophy of leadership and a strategy for survival. **Thus, the following items are humbly offered as advice for edification:**

 ✓ Leadership passion - there must be a passion for leadership. I truly believe that God has given me a leadership anointing. When there is a passionate calling, one is able to go through the rough places and weather the tough storms of life without being overwhelmed or dealt a fatal blow that puts you out of the leadership race.

 ✓ Leadership Potential – remember that you are a leader. There is something uniquely different in each person that propels them forward so that they can accomplish what they are suppose to accomplish in this earth realm. If you do not fulfill your leadership potential, then this earth will be incomplete due to you not completing your purpose on this earth.

✓ Develop your leadership skills – learn all you can about the art of leadership. Study the different character traits of successful leaders. Even when you think you know it all, study even harder.

✓ Be a servant leader – if you do not have a heart to serve others, then it will be difficult to lead them. Be willing to roll up your sleeves and perform even the most menial tasks or functions. When you demonstrate to others that you are not "too good" to labor among them, you will earn their esteem and respect. They will be more likely to follow you.

✓ Be patient, be persistent, and persevere – it took me 27 years before I achieved my dream of becoming a president of a college. Although the climb was arduous and the road rough, I did not allow my dream to be deferred. Even when I encountered what some would call career set backs, I learned how to find other avenues to achieve success. When a president decided that she no longer wished for me to serve in her administrative cabinet, I was removed from the position. I returned to the classroom as a professor. This time became a very prolific period in my life. For I served for two summers as a Pentagon fellow, and I had several books and articles published. I also helped to plan and implement several major professional conferences. I purposed in my heart that no matter where I was placed to serve, I would exceed excellence. During this period, as a testimony to my productivity, my professional colleagues gave me a perfect performance evaluation rating.

✓ Be dedicated and put your mark of excellence on every job - Never allow bitter experiences or other things to cause you to perform less than your best. Subscribe to my personal motto "Don't be good. Don't be very good. Don't be excellent. Exceed excellence in all your endeavors".

✓ Remain humble – in other words as advancement comes to you, do not get the "**big head**". Have a positive self-concept about yourself, but most of the time you will have to "check the me attitude at the door".

✓ Be a winner – purpose in your heart that you will be a winner and not a loser. Remember with a winning heart, winners never quit, and quitters never win.

✓ Be kind – remember that you may have to pass the same people on your way down the corporate ladder as you bypassed going up the corporate ladder. There is wisdom in the words "you never know who may have to hand you your last glass of water".

✓ Remember, life is not fair. Along the way, you will get cheated out of some things that you deserve. However, do not despair, because where one door is closed, another door of blessing will be opened. Truly, all things do work together for your ultimate good.

✓ Be more of a listener – there is a saying that "a wise old owl sitting on an oak, the more she heard, the less she spoke; the less she spoke, the more she heard. We can take a tip from that wise old bird.'

✓ Do not hold bitterness - When someone hands you what he or she considers to be a corporate blow, try to forgive them and move on with new adventures or a new agenda. "When handed a lemon, make lemonade."

✓ Trust God – in Psalms 75, there is a verse that says, "Promotion comes not from the east nor from the west but from God. He takes down one and puts another up". So if you trust God, your dreams will become reality.

It was a long journey from Sorrow Valley. Along the way, I did become tired, tried, and weary. I went through the fire; yet, I emerged from the fire not scorched. I purposed in my heart while living in Sorrow Valley that "only the strong would survive". So I became an over comer and a survivor. However, the greatest leadership lesson that I learned was "seek ye first the kingdom of God and his righteousness and all things will be added unto you" in due season if you faint not.

The Accidental President

Glenda D. Price
President, Marygrove College

I did not begin my academic career with a goal of becoming a college president. Indeed there are some days when I am very surprised that I am one. In many ways, my road to the presidency is a textbook example of professional growth, yet it is atypical with respect to some of the choices that I have made.

In high school, I decided that I wanted to be a scientist. However, growing up in a family where no member of my generation or the one before me had even attended college, the goal of being a doctorally-prepared researcher seemed unattainable. Good high school counseling allowed me to discover clinical laboratory science (medical technology) a major that I pursued as an undergraduate. I fell in love and determined that I had found the ideal career.

My work as a laboratory professional was challenging and rewarding. I had no plans to ever do anything else with my life other than perfect the skills needed to be a master clinician. Because I worked in a teaching hospital, I found myself instructing students. Because I was committed to doing a good job, I sought ways to be more effective in my self-ascribed role of "teacher". Thus, I enrolled in and completed a master's degree in educational media.

Shortly after completing my degree, a position became available in the medical technology program, and the director invited me to join the faculty. I was unsure of this move as I was truly happy in my job. However, I took the plunge and entered a whole new world. Teaching full time in the classroom and laboratory became my new passion.

As you know, faculty with master's degrees in doctoral level institutions are generally not promoted or tenured. Thus a doctorate became a necessary goal. My challenge was to identify a program that was relevant to me, affordable and would allow me to continue to work. Quite by accident, I learned that Educational Psychology is a discipline in line with my scientific orientation, would give me practical knowledge and skills which would enhance my effectiveness in the classroom, and provide the personal challenge that I needed to be happy as a student. For me, the doctoral degree represented security. It was the safety net that would allow me to continue as a member of the faculty. However, it was not to be that I would spend my career as an academic in traditional teaching, service, and research activities. Again, a colleague invited me to join her in the administration of our college and I became an assistant dean. I loved my role as an administrator and organizer of programs and projects. Before long, fate once again intervened and offered me an opportunity to become a dean. After 29 years as a student, clinician, faculty member and administrator in the same institution, I found myself deciding between the security and familiarity of a place I loved and new responsibilities in a different place far from home. I chose to go.

The role of dean is one of the most difficult administrative assignments in higher education. It is truly middle management. Deans are expected to encourage and support faculty and obtain the necessary resources to facilitate their work. At the same time, they are expected to support the Senior Administration and keep the entire institution in mind in decision making (not simply their own school or college). Deans are always in the middle, yet I loved it.

While working hard to position my school as an important contributor to the teaching, service and research mission of the university, I was nominated for a provost position. On the surface, I did not fit the profile of the ideal candidate, nor did I believe that I would be competitive in a national search. Nonetheless, I agreed to explore the position and ultimately accepted the position when it was offered.

As provost, I was fortunate to work with an extremely compatible and competent administrative team. Together, we shaped the institution and its image. We were able to make decisions that enhanced the academic quality of the student's educational experience and the co-curricular options available to them. My six years in this position produced many magical moments. Great satisfaction was derived from a growth of faculty scholarship; increased collaborations and partnerships; expanded majors and greater student satisfaction with their activities and interactions.

In the midst of institutional change, the telephone rang and I was informed that I had been nominated for the presidency of Marygrove College. I did not know the institution, nor did I think a move to Detroit would be a positive one. However, I again was open to a new possibility and had a willingness to consider an unanticipated conjunction of circumstances. The search process itself was energizing and it became clear to me that my background and skills were consistent with the college's needs.

Now, four years into my presidency, I reflect on my career and realize that I have never had a position that I did not love. I have not thought about my next position, but always sought responsibilities within my current portfolio to grow and develop new skills. I have enjoyed the challenges and the successes. I have gained self-confidence and developed a perspective on leadership that has served me well.

Based upon my experiences and values, I believe that it is a privilege to lead. It is not simply a responsibility or a position, it is an honor. I truly believe that the purpose of leadership is to serve. Leaders help others to succeed. Leaders influence the destiny of the institution; the decisions you make today determine who and what you are tomorrow. Leadership is about tomorrow; managers deal with the issues of today while leaders create the future. Leaders bring the n ecessary t alent together so that collectively y ou become the i nstrument of institutional transformation. Leaders are the people who find and excite the very soul of the institution.

I approach my life as a president with these beliefs firmly rooted in my personal value system. However, these perspectives are not always understood or shared, which creates some of the many challenges to leadership.

Challenges

The challenges that I face each day are both personal and integral to the nature of higher education today. They include:

Articulating and sharing my vision - to do so requires change. Change is always difficult because humans invest emotionally in people, work assignments, places, things, etc. These ties cause resistance and a reluctance to see other points of view. Thus, it is essential that the vision of the institution is shaped by a new leader within the context of the past as well as the future.

Social isolation - there is only one president, no one else has my perspective, my set of issues or responsibility. There is no one in the institution with whom I can share all of my hopes and fears. Therefore, as you move from place to place, you must bring your true friends along psychologically and emotionally. My friends will listen, comfort, and support, thus providing the necessary social connection for me to maintain some balance.

Time - for planning, for reflection; time for self-assessment, to know and be known by the various constituencies that are important to the institution. Learning to say NO to those activities, events, projects, invitations, and issues that are not central to my goals is the major skill that contributes to an affective use of time.

Understanding the culture - knowing what are the sacred cows and where the land mines are buried and how the politics work requires attention. Every institution has informal networks that operate to get things done and there are unspoken values that guide decision-making and behaviors. Success means learning the culture.

Knowing the true strengths and weaknesses of the institution - understanding to whom I can delegate, who has strengths that have not yet been tapped, who is misplaced in her position, and where there are opportunities for improvement are all challenges. Acting on this understanding means a change, which will be difficult.

Proving yourself - no matter how qualified you are, no matter that you were promoted to or selected for your current role, you must continually "prove" that you are capable. Questions about your decisions, challenges to your leadership are daily occurrences and must be listened to but not focused on. You must learn to hear these challenges, adjust to legitimate concerns and ignore those that are not justified.

No matter the mission of the institution, no matter the vision that I see, it takes passion to transform an institution. The degree to which any of the challenges noted above are an impedance, is dependent upon one's ability to manage change and enjoy the process. For me, these challenges have been invigorating. I am here to serve the students, to serve the faculty and staff, and thus to serve the college. I truly believe that I have the perfect job.

The best career advice that I can offer to anyone is to prepare for the future, but to embrace the present. Be happy in what you do, where you are, and rejoice in that which you are able to accomplish. When you do so, opportunities will present themselves for you to assume new roles of leadership which will cause you to continue to grow and transform yourself as well as the institutions where you serve.

Road to the Presidency

Trudie Kibbe Reed
President, Philander Smith College

Over a span of 35 years within several complex organizations, I have avoided many pitfalls related to manifestations of racism and sexism. Many women of color experience biases and other liabilities that can impede their leadership ability. When women of color are elevated to the level of CEO, sometimes our former experiences and credentials no longer matter. Instead, we are continually faced with having to prove ourselves by working twice as hard as our male peers. In order to survive in our role as CEO, we must confront negative stereotypes by accelerating our rate of success.

As the first female president in 123 years of the college's history, my initial tenure was marked by turmoil. Several faculty and administrative leaders were in shock because they assumed a female president could not succeed in such a complex role. Some persons expressed the notion that it was by accident that I was selected. They felt with a little time, the mistake would be discovered. Once the selection announcement was made, one alumna, who was a complete stranger, telephoned to offer her congratulations. Within five minutes, she accused me of not having a doctorate degree and observed from my photograph that I needed her services to learn how to dress, how to behave, and how to lead as a president.

Within my first six months, it became apparent that a number one priority was to prove myself in areas of fund-raising and image building. There were other obstacles related to gender differences within my management team and the governance board. If I chose not to immediately confront others, or not give strong feedback to employees, some took this as a sign of weakness (typical woman). Where my feedback was strong, I was seen as too harsh and confrontational. During this time period, several team members attempted to sabotage my goals. I was especially challenged when other women failed to support me. Some women fed rumors or spent time discrediting my actions. This behavior can best be explained as manifestations of "internalized oppression" wherein victims of discrimination come to believe the myths and stereotypes about themselves. They then act on these be liefs toward other members of their reference group in very dysfunctional ways.

I am indeed grateful that the majority of our learning community helped me to set a new vision and to claim academic excellence as our mission. During this time, both female and male mentors played a significant role in giving me feedback and offering their support. Eventually, my leadership success involved a high level of commitment and energy to the job and a priority to building community through empowerment of others. I continue to have true passion for my work and a desire to implement a compelling vision.

In spite of my gender and race, my ability to succeed as a leader can be attributed to a spiritual form of leadership. Spiritual leadership involves being attuned to the value of process and community. Both of these components are as important to an organization as are quantitative outcomes. Within this domain of leadership, a leader seeks a higher vocational calling which gives primary focus to issues of justice, participatory involvement, and the liberation of ideas and assumptions that impede inclusivity and diversity. The involvement of others in decision making and the dialogue process become the superordinate goals of leadership. Within this framework, attributes of gender and ethnicity do not disappear but become secondary factors in evaluation of the leader.

Furthermore, ethnic and gender identifications become assets rather than liabilities. For example, some persons declare that I am a woman of color who has broken the "glass ceiling." Within the spiritual dimension of leadership, I must challenge the focus being on "shattering a ceiling." The spiritual domain of leadership is more concerned with how and why the ceiling ever got placed in the organization in the first place. Such questions must be posed to determine how an organization can keep spaces organic and free from obstacles. The concept of breaking a glass ceiling represents an old paradigm. Contemporary leaders who lead from the spiritual domain must enable others to move freely without unnecessary restrictions.

The spiritual dimension of leadership has facilitated the growth of a stronger leadership community at my college. I celebrate the empowerment of a team, a successful fund-raising era, and benchmarks of academic excellence. This domain of leadership has the potential to build bridges for overcoming gender and racial differences within diverse organizational settings. If the presidency can be understood as a form of spirituality, this leadership position becomes a 'labor of love,' a passionate commitment to serve others and to ensure the survival of a sacred learning community. Being guided by such a philosophy of leadership conflicts with the challenges embedded in being female, a person of color, or in my case, both. Too often, gender and race become contributing factors toward the failure of a leader rather than an evaluation of the president's success centering around one's ability to foster an effective learning community, extend the campus borders to surrounding communities and beyond national boundaries, personal characteristics influence how a president is initially accepted or rejected. When spiritual dimensions of leadership become evident, leadership acts that are inclusive of fostering a positive learning community such as student mentoring, reorienting community thinking through critical self-awareness, acquisition of new knowledge, and the pursuit of lifelong learning skills can quickly refocus negative views about race and gender. The spiritual domain of leadership calls for the leader to refuse negative comments but to channel total energy toward positive results.

A spiritual movement of leadership becomes manifest when learners become unsettled due to a critique of ideas and assumptions whereby they become more motivated to search out new meaning within the context of a supportive learning community. The spiritual dimension of leadership revolves around the liberation of ideas for critique and dialogue. Inquiries into meaning become a major task for presidents toward ensuring freedom to learn; freedom to search for one's truth without constraints; freedom from tradition to frame questions and answers; freedom to value diversity; and freedom to empower principles of community where all people, cultures, and ideas are respected.

Serving as college president grants one a rare opportunity to inspire others toward excellence and the values of being in community. The spiritual aspects of leading require that in the midst of deadlines and tasks, one must spend time reflecting, questioning, and pondering more effective ways to lead.

Pathway to the Presidency

There are clearly certain claims made on a president such as clarity of mission, differential skill sets, multilevels of competencies, eclectic leadership experiences, and ongoing commitment and passion to the duties required for facilitating systems, people, community exchanges, and meaning-making. Many educational leaders do n ot aspire to the complexity of the leadership role of president and all of the inherent responsibilities without mentors having already identified leadership strengths and potential. Usually, prospective presidents are identified very early in their lives as having innate leadership ability. More important, mentors and educators alike enable these leaders to cultivate necessary skills and courage to pursue vocations that eventually lead to the presidency.

I did not set out to be a president. It was a male mentor president who insisted I should become a president. Following undergraduate school, my first position was at a major state university where I gained experience in all of the student support service positions. I later served for 18 years as a senior staff member with a major religious denomination. I was the youngest CEO to be selected for a position at the age of 28. For seven years, my role was to democratize an 11 million member denomination toward the rights of women. Following this position, I enrolled in a doctoral program and assumed several part-time adjunct teaching positions to gain experience in the academy. Later, I affiliated with a small liberal arts college and gained administrative experience and received tenure and promotion in one year and a half. With the combination of administrative and teaching experience, I had acquired experience and confidence necessary for the presidency.

Having served on a presidential search committee also proved to be a great gift in motivating me to become a president. I observed that the candidates interviewed had much less experience and expertise for the job than I. With other college presidents, mentors, and faculty urging me to seek a presidency, I decided to serve an (HBCU) historically black college or university because I wanted to give back to my community a gift received and nurtured early in my life by community elders, teachers, and others. It is because of the talents and sacrifices of many persons in my all black community that I was encouraged to seek higher education and to have leadership opportunities at an early age.

Serving as a college president is akin to raising an adolescent child. The "child" represents the college that can never fully grow up. The very notion of full maturity of any educational system could signal death to the organization when it must be organic and evolutionary.

Colleges, therefore, should continually be plagued by growing pains, creative conflict, and challenges and opportunities. Most presidents experience differing forms of adolescent "acting out" among their constituents. The analogy of the adolescent child to a college symbolizes the need for spiritual forms of leadership that is dynamic and reflective. Many women and men have experience in raising the "rebellious adolescent." Unfortunately, women too often must learn to survive serious adolescent behaviors within a multitude of organizations due to gender differences and sexism played out in the workplace.

It is said that women and minority persons have to be twice as "good" or prepared as white males. My ascension into the presidency proves this to be the case. My credentials and experience did bear marks of paying her dues. I took extra care to prepare for the interview through research, a position paper that I presented to the interview team at the conclusion of my session with them. My documents were replete with compelling visions for transforming a struggling institution. I recall walking into the interview room only to face a majority of male trustees. Their faces were initially bowed as if they dreaded having to go through yet another interview. I observed their body language as prejudgement. However, after the process, it was rewarding to see their heads rise with a sparkle in their eyes. They could not help but to notice my passion, conviction, and determination to make a difference. Somehow they believed me when I stated that transformative leadership begins with a vision and a strong mission that are owned by the entire community. They took my challenges to heart for they observed that I would be honest, even if it meant I would not get the job.

The honesty of the interview moved to a student forum where I was challenged to eliminate curfew in student housing. Facing the student government association leader, I confessed to her that I could tell her what she wanted to hear. Instead, I chose to be honest and direct by stating my own convictions and concerns. After taking this great risk, I noticed the student leader smiling at me as she stated that she felt she could trust me and appreciated my integrity.

As a female president of color, I want to be a part of a new legacy of leadership which is characterized by humility and wisdom gained from my journey of struggle and liberation. While our role is to lead by example, I must now empower others and motivate a new generation of leaders so our institutions will become beneficiaries of hope for the future generation.

As we slowly rebuild our leadership community that will foster a more student-centered paradigm, I am honored to have been chosen for this great task of leading a historically black college in the 21st century.

Chapter 2

Climatizing Faculty and Administrative Roles: Exploring the Nuances of Minority Serving Institutions & Predominately White Institutions

Black for 31 Years: Nuances

Cheryl Clarke

> "I was a brown ball of a chap when a lightskinned Negro woman re-
> fused to give her seat up to a white bus rider."
>
> from "Movement" by Cheryl Clarke

In 2000 I received my Ph.D. in English after 31 years of working in higher education. (I thought that quite an achievement until my younger sister's novel about post World War I Washington D.C. got chosen by the Oprah Book Club in the same year.) I am a hybrid experience. I am a first generation college graduate from a historically black institution--Howard University, the so-called "Harvard" of the historically black colleges and universities (HBCU), founded in 1866. I received my B.A. from the College of Liberal Arts in 1969, the end of four years of baptism, resistance to, and saturation in B/blackness. And that era is freshly on my mind for I have recently completed that long prose project called the dissertation. *After Mecca: the Impact of Black Women on Black Poetry after 1969* (2000), the dissertation, explores the literary and cultural terrain of the U.S. in the era the nineteen-sixties' social justice movements. After a stunning four years of political and cultural change, I passed quickly into and slowly out of graduate study in the vaunted "predominately white institution" (PWI), Rutgers, the State University of New Jersey, founded exactly one hundred years earlier than Howard, in 1766, ten years before "birth" of this nation. I still toil at Rutgers, albeit more strategically, in the fields of the Babylon we call "academia." And I can say there are dangerous nuances for Black women on either and both terrains. So, as the title of this section suggests, we (Black women) must learn and keep learning how to manipulate the very funky environments in which we labor.

Feminist activism, were it available to me during those HBCU years, was not possible on the Howard campus because of the racial commitments which excluded any others. Nor was lesbianism, really--except in the example of two women activists, one of whom was a journalist for the campus newspaper and the other a photojournalist and a community activist. The two lived together and no judgment or censure was pronounced upon their lives, because they were vital to the student movement at Howard. Little Victorian me was not ready to choose lesbianism at that moment in 1966--yet, the memory/fantasy of those two women helped me come out seven years later. They were one of the inspirations for my poem, "Of Flaxie and Althea":

> In 1943 Althea was a welder
> very dark
> very butch
> and very proud . . .
> and did not care who knew she kept company
> with a woman
> who met her every day after work
> in a tight dress and high heels
> light-skinned and high-cheekboned . . . .

In 1969 I became a college graduate, a graduate student, a campus leader, and a community activist all in the same year. I came to first understand my racial power at Howard--even as a woman. Fierce moral authority, fierce rhetoric, and just plain old fierceness period were carried into the white academy and helped to keep the so-called man at bay. I struggled on three major blurry fronts in my graduate program that tested my mettle as an Afro-American person, a woman, and someone who had more limited resources at my HBCU than my white, mostly male peers who had come to this public PWI from ivy league and other elite white institutions--private and public. Racism, racial chauvinism, ethnocentrism are daunting and subtle in both HBCU's and PWI's. However, there were definitely more dimensions at Rutgers. I had my pick of black nationalist, women's lib, homophiles, anti-war, radical hippies, YIPPIES, and the community organizing groups who sought to form coalitions with progressive students, whereas at Howard and in Washington, D.C. in the late sixties when I went to college, black women were enthrall to Black (male)ness and predatory heterosexuality.

The differences between Howard University, where I went to undergraduate school, and Rutgers University where I went to graduate school and ended up working for the last 20 years are quite stark and not nuanced at all, though quite similar in that both are public institutions with public mandates that privilege specific populations--i.e., newly freed black citizens and citizens of the state. Both places of course also oppressed and repressed the very people they were mandated to lead into the light--but that was pre-social justice, you say. Yes, that was then and this is now, and, I say, as glibly or as contentiously as you wish, that now both the HBCU and the PWI can present a very chilly and hostile climate for black women in the academy. Sexism is still pervasive, elusive and so taken for granted that it is often remains unilluminated in theory and in practice.

Making common cause with other women of color and their organizations as well as other feminist organizations, albeit mostly white. Holding an institution to its policies. Resisting the peer pressure to view feminism in a narrow way. Embrace multicultural education, intercultural relations, and what Burasci calls "multicentric identity." Embrace the writings of African-American women writers--historic and contemporary-- for lessons in nuances. All readers must embrace the women of color imaginary. For many feminists, this began with African-American women writers. I, for one, must attest to that and can claim that in 1972, I taught the first course in black women's literature at Rutgers, where I was an instructor in the Rutgers College English Department for a very brief two years. *Their Eyes Were Watching God, The Bluest Eye, The Third Life of Grange Copeland, Timeless Place, Chosen People* and, oh so many more informed not only my sense of self but my sense of the world as a place I wanted to be in and challenge. I have talked about my tutelage at the feet of black women writers previously. These are transformative texts and "necessary bread" for any black woman or woman of color who wishes to lead in a traditional or an autonomous institution. They provide context, history, and psychic energy.

Women of color are in pivotal positions--whether in HBCU's or so-called Predominately White Institutions--from which we can develop students and make our mark on the institution very much in the way black women writers have made their mark on the American literary canon.

Don't leave until you make your mark. We look more consciously to our students to carry on our traditions of community, service, leadership, and creativity. The chapter of writings which follows will provide action methodologies and models that we can utilize toward these ends and beyond survival.

Brenda Sanders Dede's and Carole Anderson's "The Case of Female Diversity in a University State System" presents the findings of a survey of "minority female employees" at Pennsylvania State's fourteen campus system. Assistant Vice President Dede's and Professor Anderson's primary focus is on employment, promotion, longevity, mobility, job satisfaction, community relations, and community service.

Professor Lynn Perry Wooten explores, through twenty-seven narrative interviews, how African-American women professors manage work-family conflict in "African-American Women in Academia Burning the Candle at Both Ends: The Organizations Routines and Person Values Employed for Managing Work-Family Conflict." The study reveals that the women chose non-traditional solutions to the conflict, relied heavily on kinship networks for support, and relied on their cultural heritage when making dependent care decisions. When African-American women enter the academy, the "welcome wagon" is never sent to greet us, according to Professor Evangeline A. Wheeler in "European Academies, African Academics: 'Sistah-Scholars' as a Model of Survival." The article discusses how African-American women, whom the author dubs "African," within the PWI, create alternative networks of African academic communities composed of other African scholars dispersed among various academic specialties.

"Navigating with Well-Chosen Oars" by Professor Ann Janette Alejano-Steele reprises those well-known "white water" challenges to women of color in authority in the PWI and aptly apprizes us of how we can wade in that water.

Wherever black women are in the academy, we must look for the ways and means to make common cause with other women--across differences, to the extent practical and pragmatic given our time, our reality, and our investment in the institutionalization of our agenda. Women of color in the academy need to make alliances on the basis of politics, not on that of sameness (i.e., race, gender, sexual orientation), especially in this neo-Bush era of retrenchment.

Perceptions of Minority Women Employed By A State System of Higher Education

Carole Anderson & Brenda Sanders Dédé

Abstract

The research reported in this paper presents the findings of a survey completed by minority women employed by the Pennsylvania State System of Higher Education. One hundred six (55%) of the 208 respondents perceived barriers to their career aspirations within their universities. The respondents also indicated that the universities need to be more creative in finding ways to enhance minority acceptance on the various campuses. Further, there was the perception that joint programs that encourage participation by all university citizens would build a culture of trust and cooperation at the universities. The respondents included Administrators, staff, and faculty. They were full and part-time employees. As a result of the study, we have outlined some specific ways to enhance the acceptance of minorities in the campus community.

Overview of the Literature

The minority woman faces two major barriers - being a woman and being a minority in the academy. Minority women also encounter challenges in the areas of promotion, pay, committee work, membership on policy-making bodies, and appointment to administrative posts. Yolanda Moses (1989) in her paper entitled "Black Women in Academe" quotes Black women saying they have to work very hard, be very quiet, and be very grateful that they have a job in higher education. In her research, Moses found that Black women viewed the academy as an exclusive social club. Likewise Black women expressed that they were seen as the person who could solve all of the problems of other Blacks and minorities and all sorts of things were dumped on them.

Minority women who enter the academic world as teacher, staff member, or administrator want to be hired on their qualifications and be paid and promoted on the basis of the quality of their work (Williams, 1985). Even if they are hired for their qualifications, minority women face the "two-for" rule. Many times they are hired and retained because they fit the bill and can be counted twice in employ-ment statistics - minority and female. This "two-for" rule makes mi-nority female administrators unique entities on the predominantly white campus (Williams, 1985).

Race and Gender stereotypes can combine to create double obstacles for Black women (Moses, 1989) and other minority women in higher education. There is little literature that speaks specifically about Black or minority women in academe but rather minority men and women are treated as one. The needs, wants, and concerns of minority women must be determined and reviewed and issues resolved for these women to have an even playing field in the academy. The employment posi-tion of minority women in the academy is a collective struggle against racism and gender oppression.

Some of the barriers facing Black women faculty and administra-tors in higher education are lack of support, poor retention rates, lack of funding and mentoring for research, inadequate preparation for teaching, and lack of job security. The leadership, advocacy, and ca-reer satisfaction Black women administrators strive for are affected in subtle ways by a sometimes chilly and unwelcome environment (Moses, 1989). "To effectively recruit and retain more Black women faculty and administrators, colleges and universities need to understand the barriers and institute policies and programs to overcome them" (Moses, 1989). In her paper on *Surviving Double Jeopardy*, Shirley Stennis Williams (1985) presented several ideas that would help mi-nority women make career advances in predominantly white institu-tions. They included:

1. Minority women must have a doctorate degree and should have a grounding and experiential background in a discipline.

2. Minority women should network with non-minority women and become their natural allies.

3. Minority women should be patient, advancement is a slow process which takes time to achieve.

4. To avoid the perception of uni-directional scholarship, minority women must have a resume that shows achievement and recog-nition by peers in a variety of research streams and professional organizations.

5. Prior to accepting a subordinate supervisory position or an assistant to position they must have a teaching area and have the protection of tenure (Williams, 1985).

Audrey Williams (1988) reported that Black women administrators she interviewed for a study at The City University of New York (CUNY) felt they performed at the 150% level while other women were performing at the 75% level. Additionally, these interviewees agreed that administration is hard work, long hours, time consuming, stressful, takes a negative toll on one's social life, and involves in-house politics. Likewise, these women felt that they could serve as positive role models, particularly for Black female students. In a follow-up to the 1988 report, Williams (1989) described a successful Black female college administrator as: being intelligent; well organized; hardworking; having the ability to stay calm; well respected by peers and subordinates; well groomed; dedicated; self-confident; and a good leader. They also must have the ability to recognize job-related talent, the ability to give clear directions, be concerned about the welfare of her staff, be able to delegate responsibility, and be willing to take risks.

Researchers Willis and Lewis (1999) noted that African American women in higher education must be more qualified and their performance will be held to greater and higher expectation than their white counterparts. Their research further supported the ideas that Black women must be better qualified, more articulate, aggressive but not threatening, patient, and remain feminine.

Dr. Barbara Ross-Lee (1993) talked about being the first Black woman to serve as Dean of the Ohio University College of Osteopathic Medicine in Athens, Ohio. One of the points that Ross-Lee brought out in the article was the phenomenon of Blacks still being designated as firsts in an area in the 1990s. She was, at that time, the first Black woman to serve as the head of a United States medical school. She stressed that she hoped that her position would encourage other Black women to enter medical academics.

Minorities need to be hired in areas other than those traditionally identified as minority programs and/or positions. Minority women in the academic community must be included in the mainstream and be in policy-making positions. They need to be deans, directors, and department chairpersons of areas other than the special programs that over the years have been synonymous with minority programs. It is assumed that minorities applying for traditional academic jobs will have the appropriate advanced degree(s) and experience.

Methodology

The State System of Higher Education is composed of 14 stated-owned universities located throughout Pennsylvania. The Chancellor and a Board of Governors oversee the operation of the individual universities. The central office of the System is in Harrisburg. The total student enrollment in fall, 2000 was 96,275. For the fall 2000 academic year, the System employed 4,648 faculty, 512 administrators, and 5,449 staff personnel. Of the total 10,609 employees, 571 (5.4%) were identified as minority women (See TABLE 2.1). Of the 571 minority women employed in the State System of Higher Education 558, located on the 14 campuses, were invited to participate in the study. The 13 minority women employed in the system Office were not invited to participate in the study.

To gather information regarding minority females' perceptions of their status as employees within the State System of Higher Education, a questionnaire was developed. Areas of personal information, past employment history, career goals, and university community were investigated.

Questionnaires were distributed through the System office to the 558 minority female employees via their local campus mail. To maintain confidentiality, the researchers mailed the original questionnaires to the System office, which then coded the questionnaires. The questionnaire that each person received included an envelope with return postage to the lead researcher at Clarion University.

Study Results

Two hundred seventeen (217) questionnaires were returned from the 558 distributed. The two hundred eight (208) usable questionnaires provided a 37% response rate. This number includes questionnaires from a follow-up mailing that was distributed to individuals who did not initially respond. The nine blank returns were from individuals who choose not to participate in the study. No questionnaires were discarded even if an individual chose not to respond to a specific question. Thus, in the discussion one may find that the numbers do not always add to the 208 base number.

Part 1 - Personal Information

Subjects responded from all 14 of the state universities. TABLE 2.2 presents the number of responses from individual universities as well as the percentage of total response. Thirty-two subjects (15%) were in administrative positions, eighty-two (40%) in staff positions, and ninety-three (45%) in faculty positions. One hundred ninety-eight (95%) of the two hundred eight individuals were employed full-time. The remaining ten were part-time employees. The average length of time in their current position was seven years and nine months. The average length of time for staff positions was seven years while the average length of time for administrative positions was five years and eight months. The faculty average length of employment in their current rank was nine years and one month.

The respondents reported on average their total length of employment time at their current university as nine years six months. Breaking it down, the average length of time for administrative positions was eight years and eight months; staff positions was nine years; and faculty positions was ten years and two months.

A variety of reasons were provided as to why the individuals chose to accept employment at their current university. Typical responses included: because they graduated from the school; close to home; spouse worked for the university; flexible working schedule (summer work optional); and the opportunity to continue their education. In addition, respondents mentioned good pay, excellent benefits, and job stability. Several also indicated the most significant reason they decided to accept employment was the ability to work with well-qualified individuals in special areas of interest and research.

Part 2 - Your Past

This section addressed past employment history. Eighty-nine (44%) of the subjects indicated they had held a position at another higher education institution. The average length of time was two years. The remaining one hundred fourteen (56%) that responded to this question indicated they did not have previous employment at a higher education institution. Of those who had previous work experience in an institution of higher education, twenty-two (25%) indicated they had worked at an Historically Black College or University (HBCU). All of these individuals indicated they would consider working there or at another HBCU if given the opportunity. Job titles of positions covered a broad range of employment experiences.

Part 3 - Your Future

This section addressed perceptions of career advancement opportunities. Most individuals saw their career advancement in a natural progression such as: promotion to associate or full professor, or tenure within the university; clerk III to administrative assistant; or to higher levels of administration such as vice president. It also should be noted that several individuals indicated that they saw retirement in the near future, whiles others said they saw no opportunities for advancement within their university. Several of these individuals said they would need to move to a larger institution in order to gain advancement opportunities.

When asked what they saw as their ultimate career goal, many indicated department chair, dean, provost or some other higher level administrative position. Some individuals indicated career goals of full professorship with a record of publications in scholarly journals or engaging in advanced levels of research. Others indicated a desire to earn higher levels of educational degrees and one indicated she would like to start her own business.

To prepare themselves to attain their future goals, administrative individuals identified attending professional development workshops and professional conferences as their top rated strategies. Other popular methods included attending training classes and participating in mentoring programs. Staff persons identified attending training classes and professional development workshops as their most popular method of preparing for their future. Faculty indicated attending professional conferences and professional development workshops as their two highest ranked strategies. Presenting workshops and professional papers at conferences were also popular faculty strategies. Numerous individuals indicated "other." When asked to explain, many indicated attending classes or completing a Ph.D. program as their strategy. Several indicated that they were seeking employment elsewhere in order to achieve their career goals.

When asked if the respondents perceived any barriers to their career advancement within their present university, 106 (55%) indicated "yes" with 85 (45%) "no's." Those who responded in the positive identified various barriers including racism, sexism, resentment from white faculty, climate does not support diversity, favoritism, small program (too many people want too few promotion positions), gender, no fairness at the institution, and president exhibits a negative attitude toward females and minorities. Several faculty members indicated difficulty with publishing and staff had difficulty finding appropriate evening classes necessary to complete their degrees.

Overall 122 (77%) perceived no external barriers to their career advancement. The few (36-23%) who perceived external barriers identified age; family; lack of relevant experiences; length of time in present position; insufficient education to match salary outside university; loss of health benefits; and the backlash against affirmative action as potential problems. All respondents indicated a minimum of five years or greater as necessary to achieve their ultimate career goal.

Part 4- University Community

When asked about how supportive of minority needs their present university i s, t hirty-four (17%) i ndicated e xtremely supportive while a n additional one hundred fourteen (58%) indicated moderately. Combined, seventy-five percent of the respondents perceived their present university to be moderately to extremely supportive of minority needs. An even higher number of respondents, 173 (89%) perceived that their present administration sees a need for and values diversity.

While these numbers were extremely high, a large number, 154 (87%) of the respondents believe that their university could do more to enhance minority acceptance. In order to accomplish this, a broad range of suggestions was offered. The suggestions included increase recruitment of minority students and faculty; faculty mentoring programs; support groups for minorities; and more diversity training. In addition, other areas needing attention were diversity throughout curriculum of all colleges; modeling a behavior of acceptance; better training for campus security personnel; build an office of multicultural affairs; focus on retention as well as recruitment; provide programs to build comradery among faculty/staff/administration; extend minority programs year-round; offer more scholarships and financial aid to minorities; provide community forums; and develop programs aimed at integration rather than focus on specific polarizing group programs.

Discussion of Findings

In considering the initial responses to basic information, it appears that the individuals participating in the survey have experienced at least one promotion during their years of employment at their respective universities. This is determined by the differences in the average length of time in current position (7.7 years) compared to average length of time at the university (9.5 years). It is also interesting that the overwhelming majority indicated that gender was irrelevant (47%) or of little importance (22%) in achieving their current position. Nineteen percent of the respondents indicated their gender was somewhat (11%) to very important (8%) in achieving their current position. There was a slight shift when the same question was asked of race. In this case 54% of the respondents indicated that it was irrelevant (37%) or of little importance (17%). The issue of race became more important as a total of 30% indicated it was very important (18%) or somewhat important (12%) in achieving their current position. This certainly could be attributed to the System's efforts to achieve a diverse pool of employees.

Significant issues appear to arise in the section dealing with university community and the perception of a lack of support for minority needs. The high numbers of negative responses in this area leads one to believe that the individual universities could be doing more to foster the acceptance of diversity on campus. Many of the respondents felt that the university community is not responsive to minority needs, especially minority female needs. They expressed that more programs should be provided that focus on acceptance and inclusion. The respondents intimated that the university communities needed to be more proactive in the recruitment and retention of African Americans, Latinos, Asians, and other ethnic minority groups.

Numerous examples of methods and programs were identified that need to be developed and implemented to enhance minority acceptance, beginning at the State System level down through the universities, colleges and departments within individual schools. Generally, survey respondents indicated programming ideas such as more culturally based programs; more research opportunities; stepped up recruiting and better efforts at retention; more social events that would attract minorities and those that need to be exposed to minority issues; and being more proactive in the larger community for minority employees. Some specific ways to enhance the acceptance of minorities in the campus community as delineated by the study, institutions began to:

- provide mentoring programs;
- encourage support groups;
- sponsor diversity workshops;
- get rid of the white male old boys club;
- hire more minorities in higher positions;
- have more people of color on search committees;
- encourage information exchanges;
- not assume all minorities are black and/or lazy;
- have open dialogues regarding issues of race;
- provide more research and professional development opportunities;
- provide community forums and outreach opportunities for locals;
- have a more concerned office of social equity;
- sponsor more programs aimed at integration;
- provide more advancement opportunities for minority faculty;
- provide more opportunities for minority participation in the governance structure and decision-making process; and,
- the administration should monitor and stop inappropriate behavior.

The universities need to be more creative in finding ways to enhance minority acceptance within their communities. Joint programs that encourage participation by all university citizens can build a culture of trust and cooperation which values and encourages the voices and talents of minorities. Until we build a community of inclusiveness, the State System of Higher Education may find itself losing valuable human resources to alternative employment opportunities.

Questions for Future Research

A major weakness of this study is that it lacks the ability to compare data to other groups or even to minority female cohorts from a different time period. Questions also need to be asked as to whether there is a statistically significant difference between minority females compared to the body of white female employees when looking at various issues included in the present study. The authors would recommend a similar study be conducted in three years, which includes all minority females as well as a sample of similar size of white females.

A special thanks is extended to Dr. Karen Lum, of the Office of Social Equity, State System of Higher Education, Harrisburg for her valuable assistance with this research project. Ms. Lum was responsible for the initial distribution of the questionnaire as well as the follow- up mailings. The cooperation and assistance of the System is greatly appreciated.

Special thanks is also extended to the Office of Research and Graduate Studies at Clarion University for their generous support for operational expenses and the undergraduate and graduate assistants who worked on the project.

References

Hankin, Joseph N. "Affirmative action in two-year colleges." Paper presented at the Annual National Conference on Issues Facing Black Administrators at Predominantly White Colleges and Universities, Cambridge, MA., 21 June 1984.

Moses, Yolanda T. *Black women in academe: Issues and strategies.* Washington, D.C.: Association of American Colleges and Universities. 1989.

Ross-Lee, Barbara. "Dr. Ross-Lee becomes 1st black woman to lead a US medical school." *Jet 8* November 1993.

Williams, Audrey. "Research on black women college administrators: Descriptive and interview data." *Sex Roles* 21 (1/2): 1989.

Williams, Audrey. "Black women college administrators: Reality or myth?" *Initiatives,* Vol. 53, No. 1 (1990, Spring).

Williams, Shirley Stennis. "Surviving double jeopardy in academe: Minority female administrators at predominately white universities." Paper presented at the Annual meeting of the National Association of Women Deans, Administrators, and Counselors, Milwaukee, WI., 1985,

April.

Willis, Arlette Ingram and Karla C. Lewis, Karla C. "Our known everydayness: Beyond a response to white privilege." *Urban Education* 1999, May.

Burning the Candle at Both Ends: Managing Work-Family Conflict

Joycelyn Finley-Hervey & Lynn Perry Wooten

Abstract

Through twenty-seven narrative interviews, this study explores how African-American women professors manage work-family conflict. Work-family conflict is defined as a form of inter-role conflict in which the role pressures of work and family domains are mutually non-compatible in some respect. The management of work-family conflict entails developing routines to decrease the inter-role conflict or coping strategies that allow individuals to balance the demands of work and family. The qualitative analysis of the narrative interviews revealed that African-American women faculty members rely on organizational routines, such as supportive work cultures and formal human resource management policies, to balance the demands of work and family. In addition, the personal values of these women influenced their strategies for managing work-family conflict. Because of their personal values, the women in this study developed non-traditional solutions for managing work-family conflict, relied heavily on kinship network systems for social support, and were guided by their cultural heritage when making dependent care decisions. The study's results have policy implications for universities seeking to recruit and retain African-American women professors.

Introduction

The work of a university faculty member differs from that required by other professions because of the unique characteristics of academic life. This culture of academic life psychologically ingrains in professors a "calling to" a lifelong technical career that demands self-regulation and intrinsic motivation. In many instances, for example, this self-regulation results in high-levels of pressures to achieve tenure within a seven-year time frame by "publishing research or perishing." In addition to research pressures, professors must prepare and teach classes, serve on administrative committees, and network with external stakeholders for legitimacy. Because of these multiple job demands, professors in many universities work more than the standard 40-hour work week (Bailyn, 1993). Given the strenuous demands of academic life, many professors find it difficult to integrate work responsibility and family obligations.

African-American women faculty members are no exception to this trend, as they struggle with integrating work and family life. Yet, their experiences differ from other faculty members because they are constantly reconciling the dominant group's career values with the family values of their African-American cultural heritage (Aparicio, 1999). Therefore, we have a need to better understand how African-American women professors reconcile the conflict between the demands of work and family. This study addresses this issue by analyzing qualitative narrative accounts from African-American women professors. Through the narrative accounts, this study seeks to understand the organizational policies that help these women juggle their multiple roles and manage work-family conflict. Moreover, this study goes beyond organizational policies to explore how the cultural heritage of African-American women professors influences their strategies for integrating the responsibilities for work and family.

Methodology

The narratives for this study were collected from interviews of twenty-seven African-American women faculty members. The average age of the study's participants was 42, and only 11% of the sample worked at historically black universities. The majority of the other respondents served as faculty members at large state universities. These women have various academic ranks and titles including assistant professor, full professor, adjunct professor, and lecturer. All of the respondents had some type of major family responsibility outside of work that included spouse/significant other, children, parents, or an extended family member.

Each woman was interviewed at least twice, and during these interviews was asked questions that were specific to how she balanced work and family. Although the open-ended interviews' responses focused on the institutional practices that helped women manage their work-family conflicts, they also revealed the personal choices these women made to integrate their career goals effectively with their family responsibilities. We did not probe for stories, but most of the interviews developed into the women telling stories of their struggles to manage work-family conflict, and how their decisions differed from those made by colleagues with other gender or ethnic backgrounds. The use of these stories or narratives for qualitative analysis provided the researchers with insightful data because stories are a common form of discourse used in everyday action to retell key experiences and events (Coffey & Atkinson, 1996).

The transcribed narratives were content analyzed using an open-ended coding process that entailed examining the data for similar themes (Strauss & Corbin, 1990; Miles and Huberman, 1984). The themes were compared and organized into a set of coding categories. We followed an iterative process, fitting narrative accounts into categories and refining categories as new themes emerged. For clarity purposes, themes were classified as either organizational resources or personal strategies employed for managing work-family conflict. The final c ontent a nalysis r evealed f ive c ategories that a re d escribed i n TABLE 2.3. Also, TABLE 2.3 reports the frequency of use for each category.

Organizational Resources Utilized to Manage Work-Family Conflict

Formal University Family-Friendly Policies and Programs

Family-friendly policies are described as arrangements designed to support employees faced with balancing the competing demands of work and family. In other words, these policies help employees manage family responsibilities, especially in the context of caring for children a nd d ependent p arents (Wood, 1 999). E xamples o f f ormal organizational family-friendly benefits can include health insurance for family members, on-site childcare, nursing home subsidies, resource and referral services for childcare or eldercare, and alternative work options. Although most higher education institutions are behind the corporate world in adopting family-friendly policies, this issue is now receiving more attention in the human resource management departments of large universities (Wilson, 1996).

Interestingly, of the respondents in this study, more than one-half (52%) of them had taken advantage of the formal work-family programs provided by their employing universities. In most cases, this involved u sing the on-site day care center/summer camps, or stopping the tenure clock for the birth of a baby or other personal reasons. The

African-American women professors in the sample chose to use the university's childcare programs for a variety of reasons:

> I use the university preschool not because it is the best one in town, but it provides me with a convenient location and extended hours. My family and I are comfortable with this arrangement.

> The university's preschool is one of the few in town with a diverse student body. They embrace my Afro-centric views. I don't have to worry about racial discrimination there and cultural diversity is included in the formal curriculum.

> The childcare center at the university offers flexible hours and a curriculum that works with my child's learning style.

The interviewees that extended their tenure-clock for the birth of a child found this a valuable university policy since it gave them time to enjoy maternity leave, and in some instances catch up on research without the tenure clock ticking. As one psychology professor stated, "After the birth of my daughter, I took the option to stop my tenure clock. This time let me have more flexibility to work at home, and I could take care of the newborn baby at home without worrying about childcare." It should be noted that those respondents who did not have the option to stop their tenure clocks articulated higher levels of stress and work-family conflict. For example, a science professor who was back in the lab two weeks after the birth of her third child expressed her work-family conflict feelings:

> I needed to get back to my research. The university does not have a liberal, formal maternity policy after your first child. The decisions are then decentralized through each department. I did not want to go back to work and leave the baby, but I put pressure on myself to complete a project, and I felt the pressure from my colleagues too. There were deadlines to be met.

This pressure to return to work is an illustration of the department imposing rigorous demands on the professor's time, and the respondents accepting these demands by making work a top priority (Perlow, 1998). Often academicians accept these occupational norms since a successful research career needs constant attention and because of the competition with peers for advancement (Bailyn, 1993).

Furthermore, this example exemplifies how the decentralization of certain human resource management policies can hamper the creation of a job environment sensitive to work-family conflict resolution (Gappa & MacDermid, 1996).

Supportive Organizational Cultures

Seven women who participated in the research project acknowledged that the university's formal policies did not always help them juggle work and family, but instead, the organizational culture was supportive of this need. In a work environment, the culture is characterized by core values and defines the manner in which an organization achieves its goals (Deal & Kennedy, 1982). In this sense, culture has pervasive effects on a firm's human resource management practices because it defines how a firm should treat its employees. The ideal family-friendly culture understands family role involvement and encourages boundary integration, such as a norm for working at home when children are sick or an alternative career path that allows employees to advance while devoting attention to their families (Kirchmeyer, 1995). An art history professor describes the culture of her department in this context:

> When my aging mother was sick, I took her to class with me. My colleagues, secretaries, and students were understanding of my situation. You can do these things in an art department. Other professors in the department brought babies to work, and secretaries watched the babies while the moms taught classes.

In other instances, it was the departmental chair that "championed" the family-friendly culture:

> Most of the professors in my department are men with stay-at-home wives. They don't understand my struggles or care, but my female departmental chair was supportive in some situations. For example, she always encouraged me to bring my son to departmental events and considered him when making travel arrangements.

> My department chair permits me to teach all of my classes on one day. This gives me the opportunity to work at home on other days and spend time with my daughter.

This is not unusual since family-friendly work environments reflect the unique personalities and experiences of those who work in any institution, and research indicates that supervisors are perceived as the bearers of organizational culture (Aryee et al., 1998; Hopkins, 1997). Therefore, the department chair becomes the organizational member that humanizes the university's response to a professor's work and family dilemmas, and facilitates the use of family supportive programs.

Also, respondents who were faculty members at historically black universities (HBCUs) described a supportive culture that showed a concern for employee well-being in both work life and personal life. A common theme articulated among these women was less job-related stress, and thus feelings of control in their ability to integrate work and family.

I left my job at a large state university and joined the faculty of a HBCU because of my son. I wanted to have more time for him, and I was tired of the departmental politics. I now have more control over my life, and I live closer to my extended family.

One explanation for less job-related stress at HBCUs is that the women working there do not have to confront the disadvantages associated with being a racial minority, but instead work in an environment that values their unique contributions in the areas of research, teaching, and service (Witt & Smith, 1995; Singh, Robinson & Williams-Green, 1995). Furthermore, because these women were not considered "tokens," they are called on less frequently to represent a particular scholarly perspective or to serve on certain university committees (Kanter, 1977).

Personal Strategies Employed for Managing Work-Family Conflict

Even more compelling than the organizational policies that support the integration of work and family responsibilities are the individual strategies that the women in this study developed. All of the African-American women professors in the sample had developed some type of personal coping strategy to manage work-family conflict. The analysis of the narratives identified three general themes: alternative career paths, non-traditional work-family solutions, and the establishment of social support networks from the local African-American community. A large proportion of the personal strategies provided examples of an Afro-centric orientation to coping and resolving problems through individual resilience and interpersonal processes (Daly et al., 1995).

Alternative Career Paths

Three of the women interviewed chose alternative career paths as a strategy for alleviating work-family conflict. These women worked full time, but not in tenure-track positions. The women perceived this decision as a way to work actively in their respective fields, but free of the pressures associated with a tenure-track position. This is evident in a liberal arts professor's narrative:

> As a lecturer, I am my own boss. I decide the classes that I want to teach, and the times I will teach these classes. I have no pressures to publish or obligations to serve on departmental committees. Because of this freedom, I have more time for my family and community service activities. I also do research, but it is in areas that interest me.

Interestingly, nearly 30 percent of all female, full-time faculty members work in non-tenure track positions, compared with 14 percent of all male full timers. An explanation for this trend is the phenomenon of "trailing spouse" - women taking contract jobs at institutions that have recruited their husbands for tenure-track posts (Leatherman, 1999; Wilson 1999). Although non-tenure track positions allow women to prioritize their family responsibilities, there is the issue that colleges create these positions to save money and maintain flexibility. Some women feel cheated out of their careers when "trailing" their spouses, but none of the non-tenure track women in this study shared this feeling with the researchers.

Non-Traditional Work-Family Solutions

More than half of the women in the study developed non-traditional solutions to integrate their work and family responsibilities. For example, five of the women interviewed were at one point in dual-career commuter marriages. With the trend of women establishing careers, the modern day commuter marriage has become a female-determined arrangement. This type of marital arrangement provides each spouse with a sense of achievement and the ability to pursue career goals without everyday family constraints (Jackson, Brown & Patterson-Stewart, 2000). However, stress and loneliness are associated with commuter marriages because the total segregation of work and family results in hectic schedules for both domains. An African-American woman professor from an East Coast University expressed these sentiments, but felt she made the optimal decision:

> I don't like being in a commuter marriage. I am tired of traveling back and forth, but I hope one day we will live in the same house. But, there are not many cities where both of us can find our ideal jobs.

Another common non-traditional solution among the women interviewed was the arrangement of a work schedule so that one parent was always available to take care of the children. Four of the mothers interviewed shared how they arrange their teaching schedules so that they are the primary childcare providers because they did not want other people raising their children. Also, the husbands of these women had the flexibility to work alternative hours, such as an evening shift or weekends. These four women were proud of their ability not to employ an "outsider" for childcare, but at times it was difficult to concentrate on research while watching children.

Establishment of Kinship Social Support Networks

For a large proportion of the women interviewed, establishing an African-American social support network was an essential strategy for managing the stress associated with the demands of working in academia and the responsibility of family. Examples of these kinship social support networks include the church, sororities, book clubs, and informal cliques of African-American friends. The use of social support networks is not a novel tradition in the African-American community. Historically, extended kin and kinship networks have always managed to alleviate psychological isolation by providing emotional and social support (Daly et al., 1995). Many of the interviewees expressed a need for kinship networks, especially when working at predominantly white research institutions (PWI):

> My church really supports my career aspirations and the members help out with back-up childcare. Most of our social activities center around the church or with its members. Belonging to a black church is impor-

tant for my children. I want them to have black friends and be proud of their African-American heritage. The church is my family away from home.

I live in a college town. The only time that I get to chat with other women like me is at Sorority meeting. It is a sense of relief to have my Sorors there for support. These are the women that connected me to the black community. They helped me find a hairdresser and a church.

When I lived in a small southern college town, all the black professors knew each other. These are the people I hung out with. We became a family for each other by celebrating holidays and milestones together. These friends and their children made my family's life bearable and took away our feelings of isolation.

The above narratives present support for the belief that the African-American cultural value promoting collectivism rather than individualism necessitates a connected-ness to the black community (Butner, Burley & Marbley, 2000). Because of the collectivism value within the African-American community, the social support network fulfilled each woman's psychological need for affiliation and served as an extended family, especially with the objective of reinforcing the African-American cultural heritage taught to the women's children at home.

Conclusion

The results of this qualitative narrative analysis present interesting findings on the strategies African-American women professors employ to manage their work obligations and family responsibilities. The majority of African-American women in this study learned early on from their mothers and grandmothers how to balance work and family, and these routines developed as cultural adaptation and survival skills for the stress associated with everyday life in Black America (Hill, 1971; Toliver, 1998). Their mothers emphasized high levels of academic achievement and a strong work orientation as an advancement strategy for professional success and financial well-being, but the valuable lessons go beyond achieving professional success. The additional intergenerational coping strategies learned focus on achieving a work-life balance through family values and flexibility in sharing family responsibilities. The core of the family values centers around nurturing kinship bonds and friendship networks that provide emotional support, prevent social isolation, and reinforce the African-American cultural heritage. These family values are reinforced through axioms that are passed on from generation to generation. Traditionally, the African American community has sanctioned sayings such as: Respect your elders - they took care of you when you were young, so now you are obligated to take care of them; and Blood is thicker than water - you can always count on them so don't let anyone divide you [from your family/identity group]. Truisms such as these are ingrained early in childhood and become the lessons that shape adult behavior. This pattern persists as children become parents and pass these rites on to subsequent generations. Essentially, these lessons are the strategies for juggling work and family. The church becomes the family away from home that assists with child rearing. The Sorority becomes the support system that nurtures sisterhood and sense of family. The black colleagues at Predominately White Institutions (PWI) become the extended family that creates a sense of cohesion and takes away feelings of isolation. Data in this study attest that African American women professors are empowered by work-family strategies that are rooted in lessons learned from a shared belief system that values family, group, and community identity.

In addition, these findings have human resource management policy implications for universities that desire to recruit and retain African-American women. Although universities lag behind corporate America in implementing family-friendly programs, administrations must began to realize that meeting the needs of their "diverse" human capital is essential to creating a pluralistic campus. In the context of recruitment, universities must begin to create a work environment that attracts African-American women faculty members. These women seek a workplace that is not socially isolated from others that share their cultural heritage or family values. Because of the importance of family among these African-American women, they are attracted to universities that provide formal family-friendly policies, such as child care benefits, alternative career tracks, and flexible work arrangements. Moreover, these women realize that the effectiveness of formal family-friendly benefits is influenced by the extent to which an organization's culture acknowledges, supports, and respects the demands of employees beyond their work. Therefore, human resource management policies in universities should seek to create and reward departments that foster a family-friendly organizational culture.

For example, universities could emulate the human resource management practices that some companies have adopted which allow employees to bring dependents to work as an approach to ease work-family conflict. This strategy is not inconsistent with the African-American cultural experience. In particular, African American women have historically held positions in the service industry or as domestics. Oftentimes, the only viable alternative was to have children accompany them to work. Similarly, in this exploratory study, women professors acknowledge bringing children to departmental events. Because women today are members of the sandwich generation, caught between elder- and child-care responsibilities, they may also bring aging parents to work with them. Even though African American women may hold professional positions in today's workplace, they still rely on personal values that endorse taking dependent care relations to work - a strategy that has not changed for over three hundred years.

It is also important for human resource management policies to develop retention strategies for African-American women professors. Given the difficulty of the professorial job and the many family responsibilities outside of work, a college's retention effort should focus on creating a positive work experience for African-American women professors that remove the barriers of racism and sexism. For example, this may entail establishing programs to facilitate career advancement opportunities for these women, such as mentoring relationships to "jumpstart" their careers and formal networks that build alliances and avoid exclusion from the dominant group. Another aspect of retention strategies can emphasize stress reduction, since African-American women professors are more likely to experience stress from workplace job-burnout because of research expectations, teaching responsibilities, and the extra s ervice w ork assigned especially to women and minority faculty members.

Because of this job-burnout, some African American women professors are closely scrutinizing career options at Predominantly White Institutions (PWI) and instead are selecting Historically Black Colleges and Universities (HBCU) - in their search for a family-friendly culture. Work relationships are career-defining - and negative relationships may be as consequential as helpful ties (Gersick, Bartunek, and Dutton, 2000). The women's stories we gathered illustrate their frustration with tokenism, disenfranchisement, and marginalized treatment at the PWIs that they eventually left. The implication is that the HBCU typifies a work climate of helpful relationship ties that empowers them personally and professionally. Women with this perspective, intentionally choose to work for an institution that offers a better "cultural fit" - an environment that identifies with and participates in a system of extended kinship.

In summary, listening to the "voices" of African-American women professors can help in achieving a diverse workforce because their stories present innovative approaches for juggling work and family. Furthermore the human resource management solutions recommended for helping this segment of the population will also benefit the broader academia population.

References

Aparicio, F. R. "Through my lens: A video project about women of color faculty at the University of Michigan." *Feminist Studies* 25 (1): 119-130 (1999).

Aryee, S., V. Luk and R. Stone. "Family-responsive variables and retention-relevant outcomes among employed parents." *Human Relations,* 51: 73-87 (1998).

Bailyn, L. *Breaking the Mold: Women, men an time in the new corporate world.* New York: The Free Press, 1993.

Butner, B. K., H. Burley and A.F. Marbley. "Coping with the unexpected: Black faculty at predominantly white institutions." *Journal of Black Studies* 30 (3): 453-462 (2000).

Coffey, A. and P. Atkinson. *Making Sense of Qualitative Data: Complimentary Research Strategies.* Thousand Oaks, California: Sage Publications, 1996.

Daly, A., J. Jennings, O.J. Beckett and B.R. Leashore. "Effective coping strategies of African Americans." *Social Work* 40 (2): 240-248 (1995).

Deal, T. and A. Kennedy. *Corporate Cultures: The rites and rituals of corporate life.* Reading, MA: Addison-Wesley, (1982).

Gappa, J. M. and S.M. MacDermid.. *Work, family, and the faculty career.* (Available from the American Association for Higher Education, One Dupont Circle, Suite 360, Washington, DC 20036-1110).

Gersik, C. J. G., J.M. Bartunek, J. M., and J.E. Dutton. (in press). "Learning from academia: The importance of relationships in professional life."

74   *Building Bridges for Women of Color*

Academy of Management Journal.

Hill, R. *The Strengths of Black Families.* New York: Emerson Hall, (1971).

Hopkins, K. "Supervisor intervention with troubled workers: A social identity perspective." *Human Relations,* 50 (1997): 1,215 - 1,238.

Jackson, A. P., R.P. Brown, R. P., and K.E. Patterson-Stewart. "African Americans in dual-career commuter marriages: An investigation of their experiences." *Family Journal,* 8 (1):22-36 (2000).

Kanter, R. *Men and Women in the Corporation.* New York: Basic Books, (1977).

Kirchmeyer, C. "Managing the work-nonwork boundary: An assessment of organizational responses." *Human Relations,* 48 (1995): 515-537.

Leatherman, Courtney. "Growth in positions off the tenure track is a trend that's here to stay, study finds." *The Chronicle of Higher Education,* 9 April 1999, A14.

Miles, M. and Huberman, A. *Qualitative Data Analysis.* Thousand Oaks, California: Sage Publications, 1994.

Perlow, L. A. "Boundary control: The social ordering of work and family time in a high-tech corporation." *Administrative Science Quarterly* 43 (1998): 328-357.

Singh, K., A. Robinson and J. Williams-Green. "Differences in perceptions of African American women and men faculty and administrators." *Journal of Negro Education* 64 (4): 401-408 (1995).

Strauss, A. and C. Corbin. *Basics of Qualitative Research: Techniques and Procedures for Developing Grounded Theory.* Thousand Oaks, California: Sage Publications, 1998.

Thomas, A. J. "Impact of racial identity on African American child-rearing beliefs." *Journal of Black Psychology,* 26 (3): 317-329, (2000).

Toliver, Susan. *Black Families in Corporate America.* Thousand Oaks, California: Sage Publications, (1998).

Tucker, J. and L.R. Wolfe. *Defining work and family issues: Listening to the voices of women of color.* Available from the Center for Women Policy Studies, 1211 Connecticut Avenue, NW, Suite 312, Washington, DC 20036, 1994, September.

Turner, C. S. V., S.L. Myers and J.W. Creswell. "Exploring underrepresentation: The case of faculty of color in the Midwest." *The Journal of Higher Education,* 70 (1): 27-59 (1999).

Uttal, L. "Using kin for child care: Embedment in the socioeconomic networks of extended families." *Journal of Marriage and the Family,* 61 (1999): 845-857.

Wilson, R. "A report praises 29 colleges for 'family friendly' policies: But other institutions are faulted for failing to help employees with child care and aid for sick relatives. *The Chronicle of Higher Education,* 11 October 1996, A13-A15.

Wilson, R. "The frustrating career of the 'trailing spouse'." *The Chronicle of Higher Education,* 19 March 1999, A12.

Witt, S and W. Smith. "The experience of African American women in the academic world." *Review of Public Personnel Administration* 15 (1995): 24-32.

Wood, S. "Family-Friendly Management: Testing the various perspectives." *National Institute Economic Review*, April (1999): 99-116.

Black Women in Higher Education: Negotiating the Cultural Workplace

Deborah L. Owens

Abstract

The purpose of this study was to examine the experience of Black women who hold senior level positions in higher education. The study begins to look at ways in which these women have negotiated the cultural workplace, assimilated or accommodated to the dominant culture of the academy, and faced the challenges reserved for women of color inherent in the system. This study explores the experience of Black women in positions ranging from Academic Dean to Provost/Vice President of Academic Affairs using qualitative methodology. Data regarding the experience of participants was obtained using interviews and examined for dominant themes and patterns. The primary intent of this study was to describe ways in which Black women who hold leadership positions in higher education negotiate the cultural workplace.

Introduction

Institutions of higher learning are clearly both culture and community operating within a system defined by shared values, shared language, and customs often reflecting those of the dominant culture. Women and people of color, although more visible on campuses across the country today as students, staff, faculty, and administrators, continue to hold a disproportionately small number of positions within the academy, particularly as senior-level administrators. This study examined the experience of Black women who hold senior-level positions in higher education. Particular attention was paid to the ways in which the women who participated negotiate the cultural workplace, assimilate or accommodate to the dominant culture of the academy, and face the challenges reserved for women and people of color inherent in the system.

Overview of the Literature

There has been a conspicuous lack of research on women leaders in colleges and universities. Women's appearance in the world is staged only on men's terms (Kerman, 1995) and the existence of gender-based myths about women's appropriate role in society limit women's power within organizations. The limited research on the presence of women and people of color in higher education suggests that their presence and the issues relevant to their experience in the world are not valued and indicate their numbers are small. Studies conducted by Howe, (1975); Green, (1988); Shavlik, Touchton and Pearson, (1989); Moses (1989) and Drummond, (1995) indicate that women and People of Color continue to be under- represented in senior level positions in the academy. White men are over represented at high administrative levels while white women and People of Color are over represented at lower administrative levels.

Unresolved issues of race, gender, and class significantly impact both the structure of institutions and the experience of women and people of color (Moses, 1989). Rasool (1995) found that Black women were generally perceived as powerless by others; Yolanda Moses (1989) found that "Black women students, faculty and administrators do not perceive themselves and their concerns as integrated into the mission, goals and social structures of the college campus" (p. 23). Research conducted by Weis & Fine (1993) identified several institutional practices that created the structures which limited the participation of women and People of Color. Black Women in higher education typically experience lack of support, instability, and isolation within communities of higher education (Pollard, 1990). Their presence, however, is often sustained by a sense of personal and community responsibility and the potential for challenging oppression.

Researchers have found few structural or cultural accommodations designed to increase the presence and value of women in higher education, particularly as faculty, administrators, and leaders within the institution (Fischer, 1975; Howe, 1975; McKenna, 1990; and Shavlik, Touchton and Pearson, 1989). In fact, research on issues related to women in higher education is limited, even twenty years after affirmative action policies designed to increase the number of women and people of color in the academy were mandated for institutions receiving federal funds. Even fewer studies have focused on the presence, experiences, or issues of African American women in the academy. Snearle (1997) and others indicate that African American women are both under-represented and under-utilized in higher education. The status of women, African American women in particular, is such that several studies have attempted to identify strategies which might enable women to become more successful in achieving leadership positions in higher education.

Higher education in general has failed to design, implement, and enforce policies that categorically reflect fair and equitable recruitment practices, performance evaluations, and promotion practices (McCombs, 1989). One outcome is the limited presence of Black women at all levels within higher education; another is the tendency for those Black women who have survived, achieving leadership positions in higher education, to be more highly qualified than peers in similar positions (Green, 1988).

One of the challenges for Black women is to enter and remain within the university and perform all responsibilities without losing cultural integrity (McCombs, 1989; Mirza, 1995). Rasool (1995) suggests that self-identity is routinely created and sustained in the reflexive activities of the individual in such situations. She proposes that Black women must understand how their social roles have been determined, culturally and historically, within society and how they as individuals are perceived and experienced within the academy to establish their identity. This process enables women to maintain the struggle for access and opportunity in higher education while challenging the barriers that prevent or limit their participation.

Colleges and universities are complex organizations. "Those who lead them play a vital role in shaping the culture of these institutions through decision making, personnel practices . . . and their own personal leadership styles" (Richardson, 1994, p. 22). Clearly, addressing issues of diversity, particularly as they relate to gender and ethnicity/culture/race, requires more than attention to employment practices (Davies & Holloway, 1995). Although there has been a small but steady increase in the number of women appointed to top positions, and the amount of research on women in administration has increased in the past ten years (Moore, 1984), the issue of institutional culture has not been adequately addressed. Women and people of color continue to be silenced within the academy, forced to assimilate to the dominant culture rather than encouraged to participate in the construction of a more inclusive culture/community (Weis and Fine, 1993).

Structural change, a change in institutional culture, is necessary to create an environment which both reflects and supports diversity on many levels. Transformational change such as this will often require a new mission statement, the appointment of women and people of color to administrative positions (particularly those who report directly to the president), the appointment of women and People of Color to the faculty and, curricular reform designed to integrate issues of diversity across the curricula (Bensimon, 1993). Several other researchers have made recommendations for structural changes in higher education which would eliminate racism and/or sexism enabling access for women and Blacks to entry-level positions which lead to leadership positions or tenured professorships. Mickelson, Smith & Oliver (1993) make recommendations regarding hiring practices and policies; Rowe (1989) details the One-to-One Approach for transforming an institution; and Shavlik, Touchton & Pearson (1989) encourage the academy to "rethink the way campuses function relative to women" (p. 445). Clearly, change in the culture of higher education is necessary, both in general and within particular institutions, if higher education is to authentically reflect and support women and People of Color as members of the academy.

This study is designed to examine the experience of Black women leaders in higher education, contributing to our knowledge and understanding of the experience of Black women who have achieved positions of leadership despite the inherent barriers.

Methodology

Participants

African American women who served as dean, vice president, or presidential associate, responsible for academic affairs or student affairs at colleges and universities in the United States were the focus of this study. Women holding such positions were identified through a variety of ways, including referrals from colleagues in the field and publications in higher education (primarily the *Chronicle for Higher Education* and *Black Issues in Higher Education*). In addition, participants were identified at the American Council on Education

Annual Meeting. Twelve women were approached regarding participation in this study and six agreed to be interviewed.

Research Tools

Data regarding the experience of participants was collected through an interview process. Interviews were tape recorded with the participant's permission and transcribed for data analysis. The decision to use personal interviews as the primary source of data is supported by the literature. Margaret Jablonski (1989) highlights the value of qualitative methods in the study of leadership and found interviews particularly useful when studying women. Audrey Williams (1989) found interviews critical in gathering data regarding the individual experiences of women in higher education while Estela Bensimon (1993) found interviews were necessary to examine women's experience within a cultural context. The literature indicates that interviews typically resulted in more detailed, descriptive information than other forms of data collection. In fact, self reports tended to contribute the most accurate picture of the behaviors and characteristics associated with mid-level administrators in higher education (Mark, 1986).

The literature indicates that we can learn more about the experience of women in higher education through qualitative measures, particularly through the use of interviews. For this study, interview questions were developed by the author to provide structure to the dialogue. Points of interest included personal journey/career path, personal and professional strategies for growth, obstacles to career development, institutional, cultural, and institutional commitment/action regarding diversity.

Analysis

Data gained from the tape-recorded interviews were transcribed and reviewed. Field notes and preliminary thoughts and ideas about the data were recorded and organized as data were examined for dominant themes and patterns both within and between participant responses. The primary intent of this study was to describe the ways in which Black women who hold leadership positions in higher education negotiate the cultural workplace. The data were also examined in terms of the following assumptions identified at the outset of this study:

- Culture of the workplace (institutional goals and values) and the fit with participants' own values, goals, and leadership styles.
- Issues of access to positions of leadership through the examination of individual career paths.
- Identification of institutional structures and practices which have impeded advancement.
- Perceived impact of their presence in leadership positions on institutional culture.

Emerging themes were also identified following subsequent reviews of the data. Themes and categories identified through this process were coded and organized, identifying overlapping categories. Summaries of data were developed and examined, examples from the data were identified, and information gained from other documents was integrated into a narrative description of each participant and a narrative report of the findings of the study.

Study Participants

Six women holding senior level administrative positions in higher education were interviewed about their experiences for this study. Interviews were conducted over a seven-month period in person or by telephone. In general, these women were highly competent, actively engaged in the academy and involved in both professional and community organizations. They demonstrated a strong commitment to diversity in their work in the academy and in their participation in the larger community. Most aspire to higher positions in the academy and recognize the challenges before them as they continue their professional journeys.

The positions held by the participants in this study ranged from Dean to Vice President and included a Presidential Associate. The women served primarily in academic affairs and had held their current positions for one to six years. All six women had been active in higher education in some capacity for a number of years, most serving as faculty and/or deans. Two participants had not held faculty appointments before assuming their current positions. All six participants worked in one of four coeducational institutions ranging in size from a large state-funded research institution to small independent colleges/graduate schools and a large state-funded community college. One institution was located in the midwest, the remaining institutions were in California. Two of those institutions have multiple campuses, one with campuses located in California and Washington the other with four locations throughout the state of California. Four vice presidents participated in this study, two with concurrent appointments as dean. Titles and primary responsibilities and challenges for all six participants are outlined below:

Dr. X -Senior Associate Vice President for Academic Affairs/Dean of Graduate Studies - responsibilities include oversight of curriculum, graduate studies, accreditation, and program review. Challenges include being appointed to a position to 'clean up' the division.

Dr. U -Vice President for Academic Affairs/Dean of the Faculty - responsibilities include oversight of academic programs, children's school, student services, extension and leadership, and support of the faculty. Challenges include small setting with limited financial resources and few support staff and the need to assume a variety of roles as a result.

Dr. Q -Vice President for Instruction - responsibilities include oversight of instructional programs with division leaders/managers, extended day director, library staff and community education center director. Challenges include providing professional development opportunities for those she supervises and shifting into a new role within the college community.

Dr. V -Vice President for Student and Learning Services - responsibilities include oversight of student support services, media, and learning resources program. Challenges include working within the context of a newly mandated shared governance system, collective bargaining, and the political climate within the institution.

Dr. V -Presidential Associate - charged with developing the school of education and the teacher credentialing program and working with accrediting bodies in preparation for expansion. This was a one year appointment. Challenges include meeting the demands of the accrediting agencies and working with a divided faculty.

Dr. Z -Dean of the College - responsibilities include oversight for two academic programs and oversight of all other functions of the branch campus, including student services, accreditation, facilities, staff supervision, faculty leadership, fund raising, and serving as campus liaison to outside agencies. Challenges include serving as the 'sole administrator on campus,' balancing a number of tasks and responsibilities with limited support, managing a branch campus located at some distance from the main campus, and limited financial resources.

The women who participated in this study were highly competent, actively engaged in the academy and involved in both professional and community organizations. They demonstrate a strong commitment to diversity in their work in the academy and in their participation in the larger community. Most aspire to higher positions in the academy and recognize the challenges before them as they continue their professional journey.

Strategies Used to Negotiate the Culture

All of the women interviewed have developed strategies to assist them as they negotiate the culture of the higher education communities in which they work. Their strategies included finding a personal/professional style, not compromising self as a woman or as an African American, always striving to do one's best and to be enthusiastic, leaving very little room for valid criticisms of the quality of their work; developing an approach to manage complex tasks and competing responsibilities, learning all they can from available resources, and setting goals and reviewing them regularly. They also discussed the importance of maintaining clarity about their identity as Black women, developing effective mentoring relationships, and developing supportive professional networks.

Mentors and Networks

The findings of this study highlight the significant role that mentors and networks serve for African American women. All of the participants identified at least one mentor who provided assistance, direction, and support in their journey. Some were chosen by the participant as indicated by Dr. Y: "I carefully chose someone to mentor me, an African American woman president." Others were mentored by colleagues who took an interest in their careers and became mentors to them. Most identified more than one mentor,

each serving a different function or serving it at a different point in their careers, including men and women residing both in and outside of the academy. Dr. U noted that "I've had a variety of mentors who've helped me to pursue my own intellectual gifts," and Dr. X commented that "mentors come in all shapes and forms." Mentors often played a significant role in the career development of the women interviewed. One participant stated "I think I am where I am because I had a mentor," a comment which seems to represent the experience of most of the women interviewed. One participant cautioned that not all mentors are 'healthy' indicating that it is important to learn to assess the advice offered before proceeding.

Participants were also asked to respond to a question about professional and/or personal networks. All of the participants indicated that they have developed both personal and professional networks to serve a variety of purposes. One participant indicated that she had developed "professional ones that you need and then there were other folks who helped me as a person." Those who participated in leadership institutes were encouraged to develop support networks building on the relationships developed with colleagues during the institutes. This process was facilitated by the sharing of information about institute participants and the establishment of computer list servers to facilitate communication via e-mail. All participants developed both workplace and personal support networks, networks with specific functions, e.g., "network of women because I think that women's issues and women's movement through the academy tends to be different." Or, "the kind related to the job task, related to my personal well being and my spirituality." All of the participants identified family and faith or spirituality as important sources of support, "I'm a spiritual person," going on to explain how her spirituality has also been a support to her on her journey. All of the women recognized the value of mentors and support networks that serve a variety of purposes. These relationships have enabled the women to validate their experience in the academy, to explore alternative solutions to the problems that present themselves in their work, to learn from the knowledge and experience of those who have gone before them, and to benefit from those with more power and influence in the system. Collins, Chrisler and Quina, (1998) found that "the factor of support received or not received appears to be critical to the course of a woman's development" (p. 224). This seems to be the case for women in higher education as well.

Discussion of Findings

Major Themes

The primary themes identified following analysis of the data fall into two general areas, personal and professional characteristics which the women held in common and the nature of the institutions in which they worked. Given the very small size of the sample, it is not likely that these themes relate to the academy in general. They do, however, raise interesting questions which might be pursued in future research projects.

The women who participated in this study had several things in common as evidenced by their responses to the interview questions. The women shared the following professional and personal characteristics:

Clarity regarding their identity as African American women -their identity was dynamic and central to the ways in which they saw themselves in the world both politically and socially. They each worked to maintain their personal and professional integrity within challenging environments. No one hesitated to define herself ethnically or culturally within the workplace. They addressed issues directly and did not allow their colleagues to be 'color blind,' recognizing that attitudes toward gender and race are always present in the dialogue and that they are more easily addressed when they have been identified. All of the women belong to organizations that support their identity in some way.

Spirituality as a resource - each woman described her strong faith or spirituality as an important component of her life. Their faith/spirituality provided support, helped them to stay centered, and enabled them to persevere in the face of obstacles, both personally and professionally.

Actively engaged in challenging oppression and supporting diversity - each women took seriously her role in challenging oppression on personal and institutional levels, influencing policy and practice within their institutions. Their support of their institutional commitment to diversity was clearly evident in the work in which they were engaged within the institution. They are also committed to creating resources and supports for other women and people of color both in and outside of the academy. In general, their response to challenges arising out of negative attitudes toward women and/or people of color is to persevere.

In summary, the findings of this study are consistent with those of other similar studies (Harvard, 1986; Williams, 1989; Mirza, 1995; Ramey, 1995, and Snearle, 1997). Although the presence of African American women in leadership positions within the academy is increasing, numbers are still relatively low. Opportunities seem to be greater in smaller institutions and in institutions engaged in transition on one or more levels. The women included in this study are all involved in organizations dealing with changes in leadership at the presidential level, restructuring and reorganization of the management structure, or significant growth in program or enrollment requiring significant changes in the structure of the institution and in the leadership required to support the emerging institution.

The culture of the work-place is changing, a reflection of our changing society. As our colleges and universities become more diverse, it becomes even more important that the leadership of these institutions reflect that diversity and that our institutions are capable of responding to the diverse needs of the changing communities we now serve. Diversity issues must become part of the broader discussion rather than something added when women or People of Color are present. This becomes possible when those holding the discussion reflect the diversity of our society, therefore the presence of women and People of Color in leadership positions is critical if we are to become truly responsive to the diverse communities we serve.

Discussion of Future Research

This study highlights the importance of continuing to examine the experience of African American women in the academy. Additional qualitative research would extend our awareness and understanding of their experiences in higher education and can provide insight regarding the changes necessary to support their continued presence and assist in defining the ways in which the academy can become more accessible for women and People of Color. The women who participated in this study have not had an easy time gaining access to and maintaining positions of leadership in higher education. All have been challenged to demonstrate an exceptionally high level of leadership ability, persistence, and integrity to achieve senior level appointments. They have overcome the obstacles presented by hiring and promotion practices which favor men, the limitations of gender stereotypes which would have them in supportive roles, and the challenge of maintaining cultural integrity in a predominantly European A merican context. Further study w ould help us understand the tools required to negotiate the cultural workplace and the nature of the contributions that African American women have made to higher education administration.

Conclusion and Recommendations

The women in this study developed several effective strategies for negotiating the cultural workplace. These women have each developed a clear and indelible sense of themselves as competent, qualified African American women; even as their identities evolved with time and experience, their sense of self remained strong and consistent. The women in this study, recognizing the importance of networks and mentors, each developed relationships that validated and supported them as individuals and/or informed and clarified their work as professionals. These women found points of congruence between their value systems and those of the organizations in which they operated. They addressed issues of race and gender directly, openly and honestly reflecting both their personal commitment to social justice and organizational missions which embraced diversity and aspired to social change. Each of these strategies enabled these women to effectively negotiate the cultural workplace.

African American women have the potential to assist the academy in significant ways as the academy responds to our changing society. To achieve a more diverse leadership that includes women and People of Color, we must consciously challenge the structural barriers which limit or prevent access to positions of power. This can be accomplished in a variety of ways including:

- increasing leadership training opportunities for women and people of color, encouraging and s upporting the active involvement of women and people of color in campus governance;

- encouraging and supporting the active involvement of women and people of color in professional organizations and associations; and

- providing empowering support to women and people of
  color i ncluding: mentoring, c areer c ounseling, networking,
  and outreach to potential leaders entering the academy.

Much of the work required to assist in the transformation of the
culture of higher education to accommodate the different world
views must take place within the institution. Developing institutional
strategies can mitigate (or reduce the impact of) the problems created
by societally-based attitudes about women and People of Color by
requiring behavioral changes (Collins, Chrisler & Quina, 1998). The
president and other leaders within the institution have an important
role in creating an environment that encourages and supports diversity. Their active commitment to diversity is required if change is to
occur.

The findings of this study indicate that the participants see the
world of higher education slowly shifting to accommodate the increasing diversity of our society. Not only are Black women present
in senior-level positions, but institutions themselves are recognizing
opportunities to develop communities which reflect the diversity of
our society and are learning to value the perspectives of women and
people of color.

References

Bensimon, Estela. "Creating an Institutional Identity out of "Differences":
    A Case Study of Institutional Change." Paper presented at the annual
    Meeting of the College Reading and Learning Association. Kansas City:
    MO, 1993.
Collins, L., J.C. Chrisler and K. Quina. *Career Strategies for Women in
    Academe: Arming Athena.* Thousand Oaks, CA: Sage, 1998.
Davies, Celia and Penny Holloway. "Troubling Transformations: Gender
    Regimes and Organizational Culture in the Academy." In *Feminist
    Academics: Creative Agents for Change,* edited by Morley and Walsh
    (London, England: Taylor and Francis, 1995).
Drummond, Marshall. "Minorities in Higher Education Leadership
    Positions: A Report of Eight Years of Disappointment, 1986-1993." *Black
    Issues in Higher Education,* March 1995, 43-47.
Fischer, Ruth. "Black, Female and Qualified." in *Women on Campus: The*

Unfinished Liberation. (NY: New York 1975).

Green, Madeleine. *The American College President: A Contemporary Profile.* Washington, D.C.: American Council on Education, April 1988.

Howe, Florence, ed. *Women and the Power to Change.* NY: McGraw-Hill, 1975.

Jablonski, Margaret. "The Leadership Challenge for Women College Presidents." *Initiatives* 57 (4): 1-10 (1989).

Kerman, Lesley. "The Good Witch: 'Advice to Women in Management" in *Feminist Academics: Creative Agents for Change.* (London, England: Taylor and Francis, 1995).

Mark, Sandra. Gender Differences Among Mid Level Administrators. ASHE 1986 Annual Meeting Paper, 1986.

McCombs, Harriet. "The Dynamics and Impact of Affirmative Action Processes on Higher Education, the Curriculum, and Black Women." *Sex Roles* 21 (1/2): 127-144 (1989).

McKenna, Margaret. "Shaping the Change: The Need for a New Culture in Higher Education." in *Changing Education: Women as Radicals and Conservators.* Edited by Antler & Knopp-Biklen. (New York: SUNY Press, 1989).

Mickelson, Roslyn, Stephen Smith and Melvin Oliver. "Breaking Through the Barriers: African American Job Candidates and the Academic Hiring Process." in *Beyond Silenced Voices: Class Race and Gender in United States Schools.* Edited by Weis and Fine. (New York: SUNY Press, 1993).

Mirza, Heidi. "Black Women in Higher Education: Defining a Space/Finding a Place." in *Feminist Academics: Creative Agents for Change.* Edited by Morley, L., and Walsh, V. (London: Taylor & Francis, 1995).

Moore, Kathryn. "Careers in College and University Administration: How are Women Affected?" in *New Directions for Higher Education.* No. 45 (San Francisco: Jossey Bass, March 1984).

Moses, Yolanda. *Black Women in Academe: Issues and Strategies. Project on the Status and Education of Women.* Association of American Colleges, 1989.

Pollard, Diane. *Black Women, Interpersonal Support and Institutional Change. In: Antler & Knopp-Biklen, Changing Education: Women as Radicals and Conservators.* NY: SUNY Press, 1990.

Rasool, Naz. "Black Women as 'Other' in the Academy." in *Feminist Academics: Creative Agents for Change.* Edited by Morley and Walsh. (London, England: Taylor and Francis, 1995).

Richardson, F.C. "The President's Role in Shaping the Culture of Academic Institutions." in *Coloring the Halls of Ivy: Leadership and Diversity in the Academy.* Edited by Davis, J. (MA: Anker Publishing, 1994).

Rowe, Mary P. "What Actually Works? The One to One Approach." in *Educating the Majority: Women Challenge Tradition in Higher Education.*

Edited by Pearson Shavlik and Touchton (New York: ACE/MacMillan, 1989: 375-440).

Shavlik, Touchton and Pearson. "The New Agenda of Women for Higher Education. in *Educating the Majority: Women Challenge Tradition in Higher Education.* Edited by Pearson Shavlik and Touchton (New York: ACE/MacMillan, 1989).

Snearle, G. "Sailing Against the Wind: African American Women, Higher Education, and Power". In *Sailing Against the Wind: African Americans and Women in U.S. Education.* Edited by Lomotey, (NY: SUNY Press, 1997).

Weis, Lois and Michelle Fine, eds. *Beyond Silenced Voices: Class, Race and Gender in United States Schools.* NY: SUNY Press, 1993.

Williams, Audrey. "Research on Black Women College Administrators: Descriptive and Interview Data." *Sex Roles*, Vol. 21, Nos. 1/2, 1989.

European Academies, African Academics: "Sistah-Scholars" as a Model for Survival

Evangeline A. Wheeler

Abstract

Even in academic climates that ostensibly support racial and intellectual diversity, women of color a cademics often feel isolated a s scholars. Sometimes we struggle to find colleagues in our disciplines with which to collaborate on papers and conference presentations. In order to help us sustain our scholarly growth throughout the tenure process and beyond, a model of academic collaboration is offered. "Sistah-Scholar" networks offer an alternative model of successful and productive academic pursuit.

For many college professors of European descent, academic departments operate as an extended family. Colleagues become their close friends, neighbors, spouses, golf partners, mentors, teammates on the local softball team, and of course, professional collaborators. When we, college professors of African descent, and particularly we women, enter this traditionally male-dominated European community, there is historically no welcome wagon to greet us, even though we speak the language fluidly and often thoroughly understand many of its customs and cultural references. We are not genuinely accepted even in today's sociopolitical climate, where theorizing about multiculturalism and diversity challenges our racist preconceptions. African w omen professors tend to feel especially isolated and invisible when we enter our academic departments as the first and only of our kind to do so. Because no supportive structure exists for us, we learn to cope and succeed by creating alternative network models of academic communities composed of other African scholars dispersed among various academic specialties.

Realities: This Mule Called My Back

During my first six years at the university, I was the only tenure-track African professor in my department of nearly thirty full-time faculty. In this particular academic institution located below the Mason-

Dixon line, where Africans were not even admitted as students until the civil rights era, there had never been an African who was a tenured faculty member in the psychology department. But, according to a July 6, 2000 issue of *Black Issues in Higher Education*, this university ranks 13th nationally in the number of African Americans receiving master's degrees in psychology. When finally a second African American woman professor was hired in the year 2000, it was only after an ugly display of unruliness among some faculty, and amid various charges of violation of hiring protocol. I happened to have been on the hiring committee.

It is a constant source of slight embarrassment for me when my colleagues gather around and share stories about their individual experiences being interviewed and hired. I was not hired through the same route as everyone else. I had been already teaching at the university as an adjunct when a tenure-track position opened. Even though the hiring committee was searching for someone in an area of expertise different from my own, being rather naïve and unmentored (as many of us are), I applied anyway. The department chair, alerted by the search committee that my application was in the mix, ran with my file to the higher-ups in administration. The psychology department, previously slapped on the wrist for not having any African professors, was offered a kind of freebie: find a qualified person and you will automatically and immediately obtain an extra, new faculty position. That's how I got hired.

It is also a source of uneasiness when colleagues talk about what specific courses they were hired to teach, because, well, I was not hired to teach anything specific, just to "be black." I was a Berkeley-trained cognitive psychologist, but that tidbit seemed incidental to what my role in the department would come to be. I was offered no lab space and no start-up funds, and no one inquired about my research plans. For the first three years, I never even taught courses in my specialty area. Women of color academics everywhere can share similar stories. Even our entry into the academy is often different from the European norm, and we remain marginalized throughout our careers.

I have the dubious distinction now of being the first tenured African American in my department. Though I suffered the usual anxieties surrounding the tenure decision, I emerged from the process relatively unscathed and bruise-free. I serve on the Merit Committee in my department and I chair a search committee. I pick up, serendipitously, certain kinds of surprising information when I read the files of my colleagues, like how their classroom observations are written in the superlative, and in fact, I am struck by the sheer number of individual peer observations members of the junior faculty are able to obtain. I did some data checking to compare the number of pretenure peer observations of my classroom teaching with the average number held by junior faculty who were up for promotion. I found that while they had an average of about three observations per year, I had two, and for a full two academic terms I was not evaluated at all, a violation of protocol both of the university and of the department. A simple oversight, I'm sure. Why do the oversights always happen to us? This is an example of our invisibility in academic departments, except when we are needed as the minority voice on committees, or when there is a demand for race-based courses in multiculturalism.

And then there was the time a former chair circulated a memo in anticipation of the first faculty meeting of the fall semester. In it he summarized the faculty's scholarly activity - publications, conferences, and the like - since the last spring and summer. He mentioned members of a group who had collaborated on a conference presentation. Although I was a member of this group, I went unmentioned. Of course, examples of our exclusion abound. In a recent in-house newsletter containing an article describing the demographic make-up and statistical profile of the faculty, there was nowhere an ethnic breakdown or racial analysis of any sort.

Within the broader community, in the everyday world outside of the academy, we encounter yet another obstacle to supportive systems: the distrust of the academy in the form of anti-intellectualism in some quarters of the African American community. Historically, representatives from the academy - the intellectuals, the talented tenth - have been looked upon askance by the hoi-polloi because they are seen as, and I use this term for effect, "Uncle Toms." It is as if we in the academy are criticized for being successful enough at playing the white game when most other people cannot. We are seen as being practically useless in the struggle for liberation of the African people from the throes of oppression, since being successful may often mean capitulating to the very culture that continues to degrade the African community. Of course, many of our nationalist leaders came out of the academy in the sixties and seventies, but I am referring here to many contemporary nationalist leaders and lecturers who regard the academy as the repository of the useless Negro who is too entrenched in the culture of the European to see that she herself is being used to further our oppression, or at the very least, is an ineffectual token. These new leaders, some of whom were educated at universities, now routinely sever any ties that they may have to academic departments. You may not read these names in the refereed journals, but they have a following nonetheless among the grass roots activists and some extreme nationalist thinkers.

Solutions: Handlin' Our Business

About a year or two before receiving tenure and promotion, I started collaborating with women of color colleagues - one, an African American English professor, another a Kenyan professor of women's studies, a third, an African American psychology professor and clinician. We were each existing on the periphery of the scholarly life within our departments, and eager to progress intellectually, we teamed up and began planning conference presentations and manuscripts focused on a variety of research topics. To date, my network has produced and published manuscripts on African-American spirituality across the lifespan, on teaching black women's activism, on contemporary mothering attitudes, on black women intellectuals, multiethnic identities, and race, gender, class text analysis. These were all topics to which we could each contribute from the perspective of our individual disciplines. Since then, I have expanded my network of "sistah-scholars" to include an African American counseling psychologist and an African American academic in education. Each year, as I meet more women of color academics, my network expands. Typically, I develop a scholarly project with just one or two sistah-scholars at a time.

It had been my experience that attempts at collaboration with European colleagues in my department ended in disaster. On one occasion, first authorship was actually slyly stolen from me. I had proposed the topic and written the first draft, but the paper was rewritten with a new first author and ultimately published by a journal other than the one I had in mind. On a second occasion my repeated requests for input into a co-authored manuscript fell on the deaf ears of my collaborators. Though both these collaborations resulted in eventual publications in respected journals, I was dubious about embarking upon a third project with these people.

I admit it. I tried initially to escape being pigeonholed as a psychologist who specialized in black psychology. In graduate school I deliberately chose a sub-discipline that had the least concern with race and color, at least on the face of it, as it had been traditionally taught. However when I got my first job, I learned that in an historically European academic institution, there was no such creature as a black professor who did not work on black issues. That was going to be my specialty whether I had chosen it or not.

Even though European and African academics may share the same profession, our lives within it can be described in divergent ways. The European academic's experience generally is of a congenial, supportive group of colleagues who all share expertise in aspects of the same discipline. In contrast, the African academic's experience is often of a broader network of colleagues who are each experts in different disciplines. Their common ground is racism, the hush-hush word avoided even by progressive groups who more openly can deal with innocuous concepts like diversity and multiculturalism.

Conclusion: Creating a Sistah-Scholar Network

It is therefore important for productive sistah-scholar networks to flourish since we women of color academics sometimes lack the support we need from within our own families and communities, as well as from the academic departments in which we are members. Creating a sistah-scholar network allows us to generate lively interdisciplinary works with depth and scope unlikely to be achieved by a single one of us working in isolation. Ostensibly, my university, as described in its Mission Statement, is committed to interdisciplinary studies, so our collaborative work is valued in tenure and promotion decisions.

There are some practical considerations in making a network successful. One, if a network is small enough, say, two or three collaborators, then everyone has the chance to share authorship, in a rotating fashion, on all papers emerging from the group. The scholar who suggests the topic and outline of the paper is first author, and the paper is published in a journal in that scholar's particular discipline. Together, the network hones the manuscript until it reflects the thinking of all contributors in a rich, multi-layered dialog. Two, the network should meet regularly to tweak the manuscript, and also to discuss ideas for subsequent papers. A sistah-scholar network will not work as well if the flow of ideas ceases. There should always be a fresh idea on the table, hopefully, an idea proposed by the collaborator next in line to be first author. Three, team members in the network must adhere to the goal of at least one joint paper or conference presentation per year, while respecting the fact that members my occasionally choose to write other papers strictly within a particular discipline, or w ith other c ollaborators. Get started by drawing together a lunch circle of women of color academics to tell them about how the sistah-scholar network might work. The scholars need not be drawn from your own institution, but may come from other institutions in the same city, or a different state, depending on what is feasible in terms of meeting regularly and sustaining community.

"White" Water Challenges: Navigating the College Climate with Well-Chosen Oars

AnnJanette Alejano-Steele

Abstract

This paper will review primary challenges of being a faculty woman of color in a predominately white institution, addressing confusion, misinterpretation, and identity issues that arose during my personal search to find my place on campus. Survival tactics for the journey include finding oars to help navigate the journey, and these oars take the shape of colleagues, allies, organizations and conferences. Finally, words of wisdom from seasoned travelers will be highlighted.

Many of life's journeys are not complete without their share of still waters and rough rapids. Women of color in higher education intuitively know that journeying on their career paths in predominately white institutions will include a multitude of challenges. In this paper, "white" water has a double reference representing perceptions of the climate in predominately white institutions, as well as representing challenging waters that are navigable with the help of various types of oars. As seasoned rafters are well aware, "white" water can be unpredictable and ever-changing.

This paper will review primary challenges of being a faculty woman of color in a predominately white institution, addressing confusion, misinterpretation, and identity issues that arose during my personal search to find my place on campus. Survival tactics for the journey include finding oars to help navigate the journey, and these oars take the shape of colleagues, allies, organizations and conferences. Finally, words of wisdom from seasoned travelers will be highlighted.

I'll begin with a letter that I received from the publisher of a prominent Denver organization devoted to news about people of color that reflects some of the major "white water" challenges in my predominately white institution.

Dear Dr. Alejano-Steele,
You have been nominated to be featured in the May issue of XXX's 10th year of "Latinos Who Make a Difference." In observance of Cinco de Mayo, XXX will print profiles of prominent Latino Americans who are making a mark on Colorado's history.... Please complete the enclosed questionnaire and send a black and white photograph by April 10, 2000. We are pleased to honor you for your valuable contributions to our community...

When I received this letter, I had a series of mixed feelings and reactions about it. My initial reaction was honor, that I was noticed for my contributions to the college community that was having impact on the greater Denver community-someone was noticing! My second reaction was confusion...because I am not Latina. I am a first-generation American born Filipina with a Latino-sounding last name because of the Spanish occupation of the Philippines. Technically, that makes me "Asian" or "Pacific Islander." I suppose I was also irritated that they didn't make the effort to find out what my heritage was, rather than making the assumption and sending the letter. My third reaction was sadness/ dismay that in their quest of finding role models in our community, they had to either cast a wider net by: (a) doing a simple search of "Latino-sounding" names, or (b) finding any person of color who was making contributions to the Denver community.

I begin with this letter because it captures so much of the confusion, misinterpretation, and identity issues wrapped up with being a faculty member of color at a predominately white institution. Although this letter was written by an organization outside of the college, it reflects much of what goes on inside the institution...and inside myself. During the climb toward tenure, there is little taught us about handling these additional personal factors that go into a faculty position. Often we are trained in theory, course preparation, classroom management and time management, but we are left to our own devices when we grapple with our visibility on a predominately white campus. We are told that it will be a challenging journey, and we are rarely told about how to find reliable oars with which to direct our academic careers.

During my own personal journey of identity development, I have become quite comfortable in living (and surviving well) in the white majority culture. I never challenged or questioned my place in academe. There were so few female role models of color during my training that anyone who was willing to mentor me was suitable. Initially I didn't identify as an "Asian American faculty member" because I never had to during my training. Now that I am a faculty member and a visible member of the college community, I have come to realize that becoming visible is equally if not more important than fulfilling normal academic responsibilities during the tenure climb.

I am an assistant professor, one year from tenure, at Metropolitan State College of Denver (MSCD). MSCD is perhaps one of the more diverse campuses in the state of Colorado, partly due to its location in the city, its commuter campus status, its affordability, and its open admission policies. On a campus of 17,500 students and almost 400 full-time faculty, 23% of students are persons of color and 19% of faculty are persons of color (MSCD Fact Book, 2000). Despite this, there continue to be challenges on this predominately white campus. These challenges parallel the sentiments of honor, confusion, and dismay mentioned in association with the letter.

Honor

When I began my academic career at MSCD in 1996, I felt a combination of honor, pride, and relief when I earned the joint position in Psychology and Women's Studies. These feelings were part of my Filipino cultural attitudes that, after family, place education and academic achievements above all accomplishments. I survived the competitive job search process in the fields of psychology and women's studies. With the scarcity of academic positions around the country, I knew that I was fortunate to have landed such a position.

Once I began the position, I was well aware of the need for service activities that would show my contributions to the college community. These were well-known standard elements of the tenure climb. Soon I was asked to serve on curriculum committees, faculty search committees, graduation and advising committees. I was honored to be asked often to sit on these committees that would allow me to learn about the inner workings of the college, especially so early in my academic career at MSCD. This honored feeling was short-lived and soon replaced by confusion. The waters became rougher and navigation became questionable.

Confusion

Once the feeling of honor dissipated, it was soon replaced by confusion, caution, and second-guessing the motives for my invitations to sit on committees. It became less clear as to what courses and committee commitments would be best for attaining tenure and how being a faculty of color would factor into this journey. Assumptions associated with teaching responsibilities, student and faculty animosity, and committee quotas contributed to the confusion surrounding role identity on a predominately white campus.

Assumptions Associated with Teaching Responsibilities

At MSCD, our graduation requirements specify that programs of study must include one course in the category labeled, "Multicultural courses." Much like the assumption in the award letter that I was Hispanic, it is often assumed/expected in most colleges that a person of color or a person who has experienced societal oppression will teach these courses and be able to convey the material more clearly than their white colleagues. Therefore, it is no surprise that I have taught three of these courses from a list of 20 - 30 approved multicultural courses. Although I did not receive extensive training in multicultural course preparation in graduate school, I felt it was my responsibility to teach these courses because I am a visible woman of color on campus and it makes me available to students of color seeking knowledge about their backgrounds and seeking advisors. The confusion stemmed from conflict between teaching courses I was trained to teach versus courses I should teach because I was a woman of color.

Student Animosity

Once inside the classroom, animosity on the part of some students can also add to the confusion of being a visible role model on campus. Some of this animosity arises from misunderstanding or assumptions that students make, particularly in the multicultural courses that I teach. Because MSCD is a predominately white college, the motives of having such a requirement are often challenged. Because of "people like me" (i.e., people of color, feminists, oppressed groups), students have to "survive" the requirement of taking a multicultural course. The multicultural course is perceived differently from the

English, math, or history requirements and is seen as less "practical," or that racism/ sexism/ heterosexism/able-bodyism is no longer an issue in today's society. Many students perceive this requirement as one additional (useless) hoop through which they must to jump in order to graduate and because of that, I represent an obstacle. The resurging backlash to programs like Women's Studies, African-American Studies and Chicano Studies across the country reflects these sentiments (Hu-Dehart, 1995, 2000). Aside from this lack of motivation seen in some students, other students may also have reservations or concerns that my courses will be "White Male Bashing" courses, or that I will be another person of color getting on my soapbox, screaming about the injustices of racism. As a faculty member, knowing such resistance consistently shows up each semester makes me less motivated to teach in a predominately white college where the waters are less than welcoming.

In addition, students misinterpret or make assumptions based on appearances. Because of my brown skin tone and my shorter stature associated with being a Filipino woman, I have been met with questioning looks on the first day of class. My educational career was such that I was privileged to continue my education from kindergarten to postdoctoral training with no breaks, and I received my Ph.D. at the age of 28. I simply do not appear as old as my colleagues who are also in their mid-thirties. My appearance has elicited reactions as subtle as uncomfortable questioning glances to verbal reactions of "Where's the professor?" or "Are you the teaching assistant?" I have been told later in the semester that one of their concerns was that I was too young to be teaching college. The average age of students on MSCD's campus is 28, and I often have a handful of students older than me in each class. Some students have also stated their reservations about my authority because it was clear that I was younger than they were, hence they would challenge my position and knowledge with an attitude. Some students get over it and for others, these feelings reappear throughout the semester in informal and formal evaluations. Student animosity in these forms has made me hesitant to want to be a visible woman of color in a predominately white college. Messages of acceptance and rejection add to the confusion and hesitancy. These messages come through outside the classroom as well.

Committee Quotas or Tokenism

Outside of the classroom and away from student impressions are the responsibilities of service to the college, often in the form of membership in committees. I have been well aware of the need to have "representative" committees reflect the gender and ethnic makeup of the larger college community. Often, the motivation is the fear of unfair hiring practices or unfair decision making that does not reflect the community's diversity. I have been told, "We need you to provide perspective for minority representation". What I've heard with these words is the underlying message, "We need to fill a quota, to represent ALL minorities, so that we're not accused of excluding minority voices. You are our token representative!". Sometimes these words are said explicitly, and sometimes they aren't, although it certainly is noticeable when one sees primarily white or primarily male faces occupying most of the seats around the committee table. I am also aware of the reality that since I fulfill two of the "multicultural" categories (woman, person of color), that this allows them to have smaller (i.e., more manageable) committees. Two tokens for the price of one.

Confusion enters this scenario when invitations to committees make me question the motives. Am I filling a quota or am I capable? Am I supposed to be the representative that points out multicultural issues and only those issues? Is my voice supposed to represent all my fellow people of color? What an overwhelming responsibility! Yet, since there are so few of us on campus, I feel the responsibility to take part and have a voice. Often the message that comes through is that somehow my voice counts, but perhaps in an oddly forced way.

Assumptions also enter this scenario, adding to the confusion of committee membership. As an Asian woman, I have been told that I may be perceived as a "safe" committee member, stereotypically docile and apolitical, chosen to serve because committee chairs assume that I won't make waves or create controversy (Hu-DeHart, 1995). Since I am not as oppressed as my African American or Latina sisters, I am perceived as someone who will not be as vocal or angry as "them". What feeds into this assumption is the myth that Asians are the "model minority", hard working, educationally advanced, and most acculturated into the White community relative to other minorities (Chang, 1998). These assumptions may also lead to animosity on the part of faculty colleagues. White colleagues may challenge or dismiss my contributions and colleagues of color may feel suspicious.

Dismay

Historically, people of color have advanced somewhat by having more opportunities in academe compared to our colleagues who paved the way not too long ago, but our numbers remain small. Many of my feelings of dismay stem from the fact that there still continue to be so few of us on campus, and that many are visibly overworked. There are the few "usual suspects" that I see on campus who are overworked and overcommitted; the few who feel the responsibility to provide ethnic representation and others who demand to have input in decisions that effect the college.

Feelings of dismay also arise when I realize there continue to be so few role models for many students of color on campus and that not much has changed since my years in college. Many times there have been African American, Latina, and lesbian students seeking a woman advisor who have turned to me as a "next best" alternative after being turned down by overextended colleagues. As an academic advisor to both Psychology and Women's Studies departments and for the general Academic Advising Center on campus, I have been able to assist students of all multicultural backgrounds. My commitment is intensified by the relief I see in the faces of students who needed to see academic advisors with faces similar to theirs.

Survival tactics: Choosing the oars to help guide the journey

My story of campus climate survival has required self-motivation and active self-preservation in the form of creating my own supportive crew of mentors. Different types of oars help to navigate different climates and obstacles; the same goes for mentors who give guidance to navigating tricky classroom dynamics, service choices, and professional development during the journey to tenure. There are about ten men and women mentors on my campus who have helped me to navigate the campus climate and deal with the mixed emotions of honor, confusion, and dismay. They are my lightposts for the journey and they represent a portion of the benefits of being at our predominately white institution. They remind me that I am building a strong reputation and learning from my experiences by gaining knowledge about the inner workings of the college. That can be powerful. I have been encouraged to use committee positions to my advantage, rather than seeing it as a situation wherein I feel like a token. The phrase "knowledge is power" is intensified when the knowledge gained is also stored in a support network.

Seeking mentors

Through the National Association for Women in Education (NAWE) and NAWE's Institute for Emerging Women Leaders, I attended several workshops on mentoring to help guide my search. The key message was to actively find my own mentors and not to wait for someone to clear their already overflowing plate of responsibilities to seek me out. M. Colleen Jones highlighted the key aspects of the mentoring role that include providing support, counseling, appraisal, information, coaching, planning, referrals, and advocacy (Jones, 1998a, 1988b). With the help of these guidelines, I sought sources of support in family, friends, and colleagues inside and outside MSCD and colleagues inside and outside of my fields of psychology and women's studies.

Seeking mentors took time and energy, and part of the process included knowing my needs up front, prior to approaching people to share their valuable time. I focused on what my goals were, what I needed, and where I saw myself in the college picture. Different mentors fulfill my needs for problem-solving, idea development, friendship, information, approval, acceptance, cheerleading/ motivation, commiserating, and advice. All of my mentoring relationships include give and take.

Besides the mentors typically identified in our home departments, our experienced "senior" colleagues, and our department chairs, this crew of characters helped (and continue to help) to navigate the larger picture of tenure and the challenges of being a woman of color in academe:

1.   The colleagues one or two years ahead have been great barometers for what is immediately ahead in the tenure process. Although they were considered "junior" faculty like me, they were those also in the thick of the tenure journey

and have been the best indicators for the immediate challenges ahead.

2. The historians have been invaluable in telling me about the history of the college, the college politics, and the changes that have taken place that have impact on future decisions.

3. Departmental outsiders have been helpful in providing a perspective from other departments on the same campus but outside of my home departments.

4. College outsiders have helped in keeping me current in my home fields, should I decide to leave my current institution. They have also provided solutions to similar problem situations that have happened on their campuses.

5. Student services colleagues have been tremendously helpful in informing me of key student issues and events on campus and in the community, and what student needs are outside of the classroom.

Over time, I found that a few people represented multiple types of support, and these knowledgeable few were very much overworked. I also have several men of color and several white women who continue to help guide my career toward tenure and provide a sounding board for my feelings of confusion and dismay. In addition to the individual mentors who provide lightposts for the journey, communities in the form of specialized organizations, and conferences also provide support for fellow travelers.

Seeking Community Support in Professional Organizations

In higher education, there seems to be an endless list of professional organizations for every academic field and arena. Often the larger professional organizations cater to a broad demographic (such as the American Association for University Professors and the American Council on Education), and although the vast majority advocate diversity, there are also organizations that are tailored to particular interest groups. For example, the National Association for Women in

Education (NAWE) and its regional affiliates (e.g., the Colorado-Wyoming Association for Women in Education) focus exclusively on issues for women in higher education. Prior to the National Association for Women in Education's dissolution in 2000, the organization had several specialized interest groups such as the ethnic women's caucus and the lesbian/bisexual caucus. Members of these organizations stay connected by way of newsletters, specialized seminars, and email listservs that allow for discussion of challenges and problem-solving on college campuses.

Seeking Community Support in Professional Conferences

Often the larger, more established professional organizations host annual conferences, and many special interest organizations hold their own regional conferences to address issues unique to people of color in education. Examples of these conferences are the Asian Pacific American in Higher Education Conference, and The People of Color in Predominately White Institutions Conference (annually hosted by the University of Nebraska, Lincoln). These conferences offer additional opportunities for networking, mentoring, association membership, and joining more specific interest groups.

Another example of a conference that specifically addressed the needs of women of color in higher education is the Colorado Women of Color in Higher Education conference. Between April, 1999 and March, 2000, I had the honor of chairing the 7th annual conference and becoming part of a phenomenal network of women devoted to this annual conference. The specifics of this conference will be reviewed in the next section, in hopes of providing women of color in other states a model from which to develop future conferences.

Creating Community Support: The Colorado Women of Color in Higher Education Conference

In November 1993, Yolanda Ortega-Ericksen and Martelle Chapital began planning a women of color meeting to address these struggles for the faculty and staff at Metropolitan State College of Denver (MSCD). As their vision developed, the meeting expanded to include women of color on all Colorado campuses statewide. The Colorado Women of Color in Higher Education (CWCHE) Conference was born, and in addition to addressing issues and concerns of women of color, it provided a forum for a day of renewal, networking, and connection among and between participants. Today, the conference continues to address the needs and concerns of students, K-12 teachers, college faculty, administrators, support staff, and community members. The annual conference is a celebration of diverse experiences and rich cultural backgrounds. Each year, the goals of the CWCHE Conference are to: 1) Explore strategies to increase the participation of women of color at all levels of higher education; 2) Address the critical issues which impact women of color; 3) Provide mentoring opportunities for women of color in higher education; and 4) Develop strategies for dismantling institutional and interpersonal racism in all its manifestations (CWCHEC, 1993). Each year the conference provides cultural entertainment that takes place during meals, during social events, or during interactive workshops. These entertainment events have included video presentations and award-winning musical, theatrical, and dance groups from a range of ethnic backgrounds. In addition, each year conference participants contribute to the making of the annual conference quilt as a symbol of diversity and unity of the Colorado Women of Color in Higher Education. The decorations of the quilt blocks range from participants' names to elaborate words of wisdom to be shared for future conference participants. These 8' x 5' quilts are a beautiful reminder of conferences past and are proudly displayed each year.

Conference Planning

Planning for the conference begins one year prior to the event, and during this year, networking fosters relationships on the campus of the hosting institution. This allows conference chairs and committee members to learn from each other about the inner workings and politics of the institution. Alliances are developed and strengthened throughout the planning process, creating networks to help each individual navigate the campus climate. Conference chairs of the hosting institutions also become part of the statewide network of women committed to the conference, to ensure continuity from year to year.

Each year, the conference is sustained by the boundless energy and efforts of volunteers committed to continuing the Colorado tradition. These volunteers are administrators, faculty, staff, and students from a variety of ethnic backgrounds, including white women allies. Planning takes the efforts of many committees (finance, logistics, workshops, events [cultural and dining], registration, and public relations) to provide a conference to meet the needs of a diverse group of Colorado women. In addition to the volunteer contributions by committee members, financial support for the conference depends, in part, on the host institution invested in supporting cultural and professional development programs for its employees. Financial support is also provided by the other Colorado higher education institutions, diversity grants, registration fees, t-shirt sales, and community/ corporate sponsorships. A budget of upwards of $25,000 is needed to provide a conference for 300 - 400 participants.

Conference Programming

The conference program reflects the various needs of women of color in higher education at all levels. Keynote speakers set the tone throughout the conference, and have included women from a range of ethnic backgrounds with a variety of higher education experiences. Each year they offer uplifting and encouraging words of unity, wellness, and hopes for future directions. Once the keynoters set the conference tone, workshops are provided throughout the day that reflect the keynote messages and the following topic areas: career and educational enhancement; personal enrichment; networking, alliances and coalitions; multiculturalism without tokenism; creating our own space; activism; celebration in the arts; and campus climate and survival. Workshop presenters are recruited through a call for papers that are then reviewed by the program committee. Special care is taken to offer workshops that address a wide range of issues for students, faculty, staff, and administrators.

Each year the Colorado Women of Color in Higher Education Conference reminds us of our goals and our place in the higher education system. It allows us to listen, learn, and teach others by nurturing personal growth. It allows us to reflect upon our strength in unity; where we've been, how far we've come, and the future challenges still ahead. Have we mentored our sisters? Have we developed effective strategies for dismantling institutional and interpersonal racism? Have we learned from the experiences of those who paved the way before us? Are we currently supporting those who will follow us in the future? Annually, we are reminded that we are not alone in our predominately white institutions. We are a part of a powerful network of strong, united women.

Words of wisdom from seasoned journeywomen

Each of the network mechanisms mentioned above have supported my primary goal of self-preservation during the climb to tenure in a predominately white institution. My support crew has helped me to navigate and survive the journey toward tenure. They helped me to steer through "white" water rapids, suggested alternate routes of passage, and celebrated when the waters were blissfully calm. I have been supported by this crew and have taken their advice to take advantage of opportunities (no matter the motivations); to use the Asian stereotype to my advantage; and to use my voice. Through the years I have collected the following valuable pieces of navigational advice:

1. **Become visible and well-networked on and off campus**

   • Develop a cadre of mentors and allies across campus, in all areas of the college (staff, administrators, chairs, deans, vice presidents, student affairs, academic advising, faculty, etc.);

   • let students and colleagues know you are there to support efforts of women of color by participating in specific diversity committees and programs;

   • watch each other's backs and support each other; and

   • join organizations and participate in conferences to support your positioning on campus.

2. **Learn to read the climate of your campus** (i.e. politics, power structures, alliances, etc.). Collect the opinions and observations of many before taking action.

3. **Pull others up as you climb.** Be sure to provide mentorship for those following on the same journey.

line of tolerance or decide to leave.

5. Most importantly, **balance work and home life** by keeping priorities in perspective.

- Be selective where to aim your energies; preserve solitary time;

- say no to overcommitment; and

- keep your spirituality intact (in whatever form that takes).

These words of wisdom are posted in various forms in my office, among pictures of my husband and son. They are words from a collective group of women role models who have helped pave the way for me today, a nd t hose c omforting words o f e ncouragement o ften h elp during times when the tenure journey has taken me through "white" water rapids. Since receiving the letter mentioned at the beginning of this chapter, I have framed it as a reminder of the challenges past and those yet unseen. I no longer take offense at its well-intentioned efforts; it is a reminder that I belong to a relatively small group of people of color in academe, and that I must continue to be visible and help to navigate the way for those following in my wake.

References

Chang, C. "Streets of Gold: The Myth of the Model Minority" in *Rereading America: Cultural contexts for critical thinking and writing, 4th Ed.* Edited by G. Colombo, R. Cullen & B. Lisle (Boston, MA: Bedford Books, 1998).

Colorado Women of Color in Higher Education. Program for the Fourth Annual Colorado Women of Color in Higher Education Conference, Colorado Springs, CO, 1993.

Hu-DeHart, E. "The Undermining of Ethnic Studies." *Chronicle of Higher Education*, October 20, Section 2 (1995).

Hu-DeHart, E. "The diversity project: Institutionalizing multiculturalism or managing differences?" *Academe*, 86 (5): 39 – 42 (2000).

Jones, M.C. *Mentoring*. Institute for Emerging Women Leaders, National Association for Women in Education, College Park, MD, (1997).

Jones, M.C. Networking strategies for trailblazers, squatters, and other settlers in academe. Advancing Women in Higher Education Conference, National Association for Women in Education, Baltimore, MD., (1998).

Metropolitan State College of Denver. MSCD Fact Book, Office of Institutional Research, Metropolitan State College of Denver. Denver, CO, (2000).

Chapter 3

The Department Chair Dichotomy: Balancing Faculty and Administration

Confessions of An Acting Chair

Judi Moore Latta

No one bothered to tell me I would need to know how to juggle. No one said that I would have to be able to find some missing dollars from an undersized budget, forestall a potential student suicide, soothe a colleague's wounded ego, write an evaluation that would determine a person's future, pick up paper from a trashed out class-room, and go to three meetings (two of which were unnecessary) within one ten-hour workday. No one said this would be typical. In fact, when my colleagues persuaded me to accept the position of Act-ing chair of our department, they said, "It's only for a little while," and "It won't be too bad." They were wrong on both counts. Five months has seemed like an eternity and "bad," I've learned, is only a relative term.

Serving as chair of a department within the academy is more than a notion. It means existing in a kind of not-clearly-defined-hinterland. In an environment where students are the primary custom-ers/learners, where faculty are those principally responsible for pur-veying knowledge, where staff carry out rules and procedures, and where senior administrators (deans, vice presidents, provosts, etc) make bottom line decisions, the department chair must serve all.

Positioned in "middle management," her role is that of accountant, cheerleader, mother/confessor, watchdog, mediator, visionary, and staff sergeant. As such, she is at once an advocate for change and a stickler for the status quo, the one who attempts to prevent chaos and struggles to prevent complacency. The department chair must give and take orders, protect people in the margins, and push others to the boundaries – and, in the process, maintain her own sanity.

If I've learned anything in this short few months, it is that a department chair will be called upon to plug up holes in long-standing problems and to address systems with perpetual weaknesses – and in every case she will be expected to get the job done "yesterday." No excuses, no regrets accepted.

It is a lonely role not to be dismissed or taken lightly. True, the chair does not have the entire university's organization to consider at her every move as would a president; neither does she have every lesson to consider in a course as would a classroom teacher; nor does she have every line to type on a service request as would a secretary; nor is she expected to know all of the answers on every test as is a student. Yet, she is expected to understand each of these perspectives. The demand is even greater when she is a woman of color in what is traditionally considered a male bastion, at least partly because compassion is expected to be her watchword. Those who have been at this business longer than I say there is a way to be compassionate and, at the same time, not be overworked. They say there is a way to consider other people and keep from going overboard on behalf of your department, spending too many late nights buried in paper and too many early mornings buried in phone calls. I am still new at this, and as such have not quite mastered it yet.

But with all of the shortcomings, demands, headaches that come with this appointment, it is still a position of power and privilege. It is as department chair, for example, that you can see relief in the eyes of the needy junior when you tell her she has won a departmental scholarship, or that you decide to give a faltering student a second chance, or that you can recommend a new hire who will raise the energy level of the faculty, or that you can launch a plan on paper that ends up working in a classroom.

The essays in this section offer perspectives and advice on what it means to be a woman of color who is in a position of power in the world of higher education. Although the views vary, the consensus is clear: chairing a department has its challenges as well as its finer moments.

In the Middle of the Vanguard: Women of Color Bridging Roles as Faculty

Emma T. Lucas

Abstract

Women of color faculty administrators in predominantly white institutions confront multiple role dualities. They often find themselves in the middle between senior administrators and faculty whom they represent, the advancement of themselves as scholars and administrators, the blending of community service and scholarship, conflicting gender roles, and minority roles within gender categorizations. Although the clash of such multiple roles is sometimes difficult, competent leadership and confidence can make a difficult job more manageable. As members of a predominantly white work environment, women of color must realize that several struggles persist within the ambiance of racism and sexism. These may not always be conquered, but with carefully identified enabling strategies they can be successfully confronted. This paper identifies the tracking of advancement from faculty to faculty administrator and the dichotomy that results as a scholar administrator.

Introduction

I am my family's first college graduate. Because of my parent's strong child rearing practices, I always expected to make "something of my life." During my teenage years, I realized the value of an education and set college as my goal. I recall my parent's comment, "We do not want you to have to work as hard as we work." Reflecting on their work ethic has truly been a motivator for me, and remembering their hard work and the racist system under which they struggled has been a sustaining force when obstacles and difficulties are confronted.

The Matter of Skin Color

Diversity, African American Woman, ABD, Talented: these were among the qualities I would bring to my new work environment at a small liberal arts college. Initially, I was brought on as the director of the Black Studies Program, and within two years, I was promoted to an administrative position while keeping all the initial responsibilities. It is now twenty-five years later, and my entire professional career has been in predominantly white institutions of higher education. The majority of these years have been at the middle management level as department head, assistant then associate vice president for academic affairs, and now, by personal choice, division head. During these years of being 'in the middle," a faculty member and a middle management administrator, I was cognizant that the job title was not protected from critical eyes and discriminating minds. I could never forget the fact that my work efforts were scrutinized by the administration, white colleagues, and in some cases, students (most often minority students), in ways that white women and men were not. As the lone woman-of-color administrator for years, I assigned myself the duty of working to make sure more people of color would join me. This is one of those items that did not appear in my job description, but I concluded that I should add this to my job responsibilities since it didn't seem to be a priority for other administrators or faculty members. I often reminded my colleagues that other qualified people of color existed when searches were conducted. This was done in the hope that academicians of color would possibly bring with them a sense of connectedness that would lessen the atmosphere of isolation I was so keenly aware of both personally and professionally.

Individuals who are uncomfortable with women of color being in higher administrative roles will test the system. This can be done in many ways. I experienced this on numerous occasions when my decisions were challenged. When exercising my decision-making authority and exploring considerations that were fair, I was generally confident of my actions. But, other challenges to one's authority often come when someone attempts to "go over one's head." I remember this happening occasionally. Luckily, the senior officer above me recognized my areas of responsibility by informing the challengers that issues were within my administrative purview. These actions provided critical levels of support that indicated lines of authority would be observed.

Women in academe, generally, are a minority, and women of color in academe are a minority within a minority. In the case of African-American women, a college or advanced degree and career advancement signaled another layer of obstacles to be faced (Higginbotham, 1994). For these and other women of color, occupational positions were steeped in racism and sexism. Ingrained beliefs and practices about the capabilities of women of color masked employment and advancement opportunities. These same concerns surfaced in a study by Turner, Sotello, Myers, and Creswell (1999), who also reported that faculty of color in the Midwest found unsupportive and unwelcoming work environments that were punctuated with racial and ethnic biases. We cannot escape subtle, and not-so-subtle racism, and many women of color have learned survival strategies that work for them under various challenges.

A Sandwiched Position

As individuals with identified leadership skills, women of color are compelled to perform a duality of roles: as scholar/teacher, administrator, role model, and community citizen. This sandwiched position is a precarious one; one that requires service as an intermediary between administration and faculty. One realizes that when it is convenient for either side, she is viewed as being more a part of one than the other.

At one level, to be an academic scholar in the institution is a challenge in itself, requiring negotiating tenure and survival strategies unlike white counterparts. As administrator, one is placed within the crucible of negotiating with predominantly senior white male administrators who have their own preconceived ideas about role expectations. The duties and responsibilities of women of color faculty administrators under these circumstances must still conform to the highest expectations of scholarship. For example, they must still meet the highest requirements for tenure and job security through research, publication, and college service. They are also expected to excel in grantsmanship as a demonstration of scholarly academic leadership within the institution. This is an inescapable aspect of leadership growth and accomplishment in the academy. This is often done as new paths are carved for possible career advancement, and they are continually confronted with the dynamic challenges of academic trailblazing. But, these women of color scholars are merely human beings with families, friends, private lives, and other personal self-fulfillment needs and aspirations. We are also not devoid of fundamental spiritual and social needs.

Therefore, ordinarily defined roles require fulfillment, like these normal and natural ones under higher expectation models of thought. Time must be devoted to personal fulfillment and satisfaction, as well as relaxation and recreation.

A professional requirement for the faculty administrators is the setting of job priorities, especially program planning, budgeting, and strategy execution. Often the faculty administrator is a generalist manager/professional. Daily activities are multifaceted, and the best-made plans must include some degree of flexibility. From committee and administrative meetings, to teaching, to student contacts, to academic planning, to interacting with colleagues, the day's agenda is full. While many hours are required to fulfill all responsibilities, they may run outside the usual 9 to 5 schedule.

In either role, professional connectedness demands the highest levels of skillin colleagueship throughout high scale professional dealings. These include faculty mentoring, academic short- and long-term planning, program innovations, disciplinary specialization, academic diplomat, and visionary qualities far in excess of average expectations. All of these are carried out within the ambiance of racial and gender conundrums. These are juggling acts of the knowing professional, and require full practical knowledge of self-limitations of the scholar/administrator. Stretching one's self in so many directions leads to a gradual descent of performance unless the scholar can focus at all times on the best strategies for negotiating such recurring self and professional limitations. At this level, women must discard a desire to be the "super person" and focus on the spiritual and physical self. In other words, the dangers of being too-thinly spread are real for many women of color faculty administrators. Women of color who meet the challenges of scholar/administrators are compelled to live in a glass house; we are on permanent display by all actors in the institutional structure. Women-of-color faculty administrators are often viewed with jaundiced eyes. A degree of recurring uncertainty remains about how successfully one meets the challenges and expectations of such a position.

Proactive actions help one to cope with isolation within the academy. By seeking supportive camaraderie within and outside one's institution, feelings of isolation may be lessened. With the technology that is available today, distance is not an issue and contact can be on a regular basis. If possible, identifying someone within a reasonable distance would allow for "sister gatherings" over lunch, dinner, or a movie. Face-to-face contacts can provide greater satisfaction. After identifying a senior fellow faculty administrator at a local university, we agreed to meet monthly over lunch. She became my sounding board, and I became hers. We shared freely and focused not only on what was happening with us, but also what was going on in high education and the world in general. These gatherings always left me feeling refreshed and ready to face the world I had left behind for a few hours. I also identified a prominent figure who was a senior U.S. State Department officer as a mentor. Although we did not talk often, I followed her career and read whatever I could find that was written about her. These distant contacts assured me that she was able to endure, n ot because h er environment w as f ree of racism and sexism, but because of inner strength, vision, and talent.

A View from Outside the Academy

Women of color are compelled, as well, to perform leadership functions and responsibilities beyond the academic setting. Service demands put women of color in the forefront of community responsibilities and general societal leadership duties. But, our singular identities in these latter roles are a direct extension of our academic training and positions. We cannot focus on our academic distinctions alone, primarily because these distinctions come directly from our community standing and general community expectations. The view of these community engagements as efforts to "give back" represent an individual desire to connect to a more friendly and accepting community while expressing levels of appreciation and other sentiments. Community expectations bring distinction and demands on already squeezed and stretched schedules. However, the personal satisfaction obtained and interactions with "the people" are therapeutic in nature.

In many instances, the white community, and the individual administrators' own community, believes it should be served. Many times, talented and competent faculty administrators are called upon to provide services in a number of ways, including serving on committees, boards, and making presentations. By virtue of one's skills and competence, we are approached repeatedly to be a representative of our racial, ethnic, or gender group. Women of color, unlike our white counterparts, come to these mandated non-academic leadership responsibilities precisely because we have distinguished ourselves in academic roles. This, therefore, gives us a more strenuous canvas on which to perform not easily integrated leadership functions. Scholars of color are requested to perform these roles of distinction in predominantly white institutions and organizations. We cannot climb the academic ladder alone, without an awareness of the many pulls on us as academics. Layers of responsibilities and psychological challenges are loaded on top of one another. This professional role duality represents the classic case of the loneliness of the "long distance runner." The loneliness is multifaceted along racial, gender, and professional lines. Intellectual and psychological expectations are geared in such a way that they are ratcheted up by the race factor. Calls for other necessary supportive faculty and scholarship roles for women of color across academia include tasks that promote growth development and achievement not only for themselves, but also for those with whom they have contact. Mentoring junior faculty is an expected part of academic leadership at the department and division levels.

The Student Connection

Yet another layer further compounds the already-identified roles. This scholar/administrator is a role model, and maybe a confidant too, to students across gender and race. Some students are more focused and can readily identify areas of concern which makes assisting them easier. Instances occur when the faculty administrator must struggle to understand the needs of different students in general, but all of this also requires more effort to understand the needs of students of color in particular. Accomplishing this in a way that will not degenerate into racial or gender preferencing requires another struggle in itself. Women of color in academe must constantly perform at the height of human professional objectivity and neutrality. This calls for an almost super-human feat. As individuals, we must be cautiously cognizant of the need to do this for all students in general, and students of color in particular, whose needs and experiences in such institutions carry additional dimensions that affect their academic performance levels. Racial bias is not reserved for either the woman or student of color, but rather both are subjected to the same unfriendly forces.

The Rewards

The appointment to a position of leadership is a reward in and of itself. This is a recognition of professional qualifications and leadership capabilities by both colleagues within the department or division as well as by the college-wide administration. This is also a confirmation of leadership capabilities within the discipline, the academy, and beyond it. However, these rewards are not without their costs and challenges, especially for women of color in a predominantly white institution.

These facts notwithstanding, my being in a middle-level administrative position enabled me to influence critical decisions. This active participation resulted in the recognition of students in general, and on several occasions, students of color in particular. These students are being considered and recognized in ways that may have slipped by because of subtle oversights that ultimately would have benefited white students only to the disadvantage of students of color. Such well deserved considerations should not degenerate into preferential treatment for either white students or students of color.

Student achievement and success are special intangible rewards, especially when students themselves recognize and acknowledge my role in their college education. Realizing that one's contributions are appreciated helps to put professional struggles and institutional pressures into perspective. One's presence, therefore, is recognized and valued, even though such value may not always be acknowledged and/or embraced openly by the entire institution. A caring and understanding yet fair faculty administrator models an environment in which dreams are formed and realized. This form of role modeling involves not only behavioral attributes, but also a fostering of creative and clear thinking, discovery, and other challenges, as well as the affirmation of personal values. However, these types of rewards often mask some of the daily struggles that are a part of the work environment.

Conclusion

This essay has focused special attention on the dualities and multiple roles in the lives of professional women of color who fill sensitive academic leadership positions. The size, location, public or private, single sex or coeducational elements that shape the professional environment of the role dualities confronting such women of color scholars really cast us as super role models across multifaceted career possibilities. Such roles are full of drama and tension, as well as ever-shifting uncertainties that are always to be harmonized with clashing personal, professional, family, public, and community responsibilities and expectations.

Any scholar who occupies such a position cannot always be sure objective standards of professional conduct will ever fully optimize all of the clashing challenges to be confronted. In the end, the scholar/administrator must continue to struggle to produce the best in such ever-challenging, constantly changing environments. No person should ever feel overly comfortable or confident while performing such responsibilities. In circumstances like these, what starts out as a negative force can be turned into enabling positive assets for the emancipation of the human spirit of professional women of color. My strong work ethic acquired as a result of such struggles strengthened the enlarging empowerment that was taught many years earlier by caring, nurturing parents who, it turns out, may have anticipated unbeknownst to us many of the unfolding obstacles that the future held.

References

Higginbotham, E. "Black professional women: Job ceilings and employment sectors." in *Women of Color in U.S. Society*, edited by M. Zinn and B. Dill (Philadelphia: Temple University Press, 1994).

Turner, C., V. Sotello, S. Myers and J. Creswell. "Exploring underrepresentation: The case of faculty of color in the Midwest." *Journal of Higher Education* 70 (1): 27-59 (1999).

The Challenges of Chairing the Academic Department

Gladys J. Willis

Abstract

Chairing the academic department at a college or university can be one of the most rewarding experiences of an academic career. To achieve optimal success, the department chair must take seriously five basic responsibilities: 1) curriculum development, 2) curriculum assessment, 3) faculty recruitment, 4) clarification of departmental policies and procedures, and 5) the promotion of academic excellence. That which contributes most to the fulfillment of these responsibilities is the chair's ability to be an effective human relations person. The department chair position does indeed provide valuable experience for moving into higher positions in college and university administration.

The Challenges of Chairing the Academic Department

In August 1977, I was invited to Lincoln University in Pennsylvania to serve as Chairperson of the English Department. Although I had taught on a college level for approximately seven years, I had never served as a department chair, and, therefore, had no on-the-job experience. I was an attractive candidate because of my college teaching experience and because I was a recent Ph.D. from Princeton University, with the distinction of being the first Black American to receive a Ph.D. in English from this most prestigious institution. The only relevant experience that I could bring to the position was my experience of working with three different department chairs during my college teaching career—at Cheyney State College in Pennsylvania, Rider College in New Jersey, and City University of New York (at BMCC)—and serving as an Education Representative for the Pennsylvania Human Relations Commission. From the three chairs under whom I served, I had learned much just in observing their individual styles of management and was able to develop my own style of chairing the department. From the Pennsylvania Human Relations Commission, I brought with me extensive knowledge about litigation and legal procedures. Fortunately, these experiences in academe and state government became invaluable to me as a department chair. However, as I look back to 1977, I will always be grateful for the opportunity given to me by the late Dr. Herman R. Branson, then President of Lincoln University, to serve as a department chair at the oldest HBCU in the United States and make a significant difference in the higher education of Black American students.

As a new department chair, my first order of business was to make a serious attempt to develop some esprit de corps within the department, for those were the worst of times at Lincoln as well as in the English Department. I walked into a troubled department, and, as someone from the outside, I was not accepted by all members of the department or the university community. The campus was polarized, and there I was with a job to do. What does a new chair do under such circumstances? I accepted the situation as a challenge, but it took approximately eight years before the department began to make strides toward improved morale and improved cooperation.

Now, based on twenty-three years of service as a department chair, I am convinced that the department chair sets the tone for the department and must take responsibility for leading the department in developing its mission, vision and objectives – all of which should complement those of the respective university. Aside from this responsibility, the department chair must, with the assistance of department members, be held accountable for curriculum development, curriculum assessment, recruitment of outstanding and effective faculty members, faculty evaluation and accountability, clarification of departmental policies and procedures, initiation of faculty development strategies, and the promotion of academic excellence among students. Without an understanding of these responsibilities, a department chair's success will be limited.

First, the quality of curricula for major program offerings is crucial. The curriculum for a particular program gives the department its raison d'etre. Students must be perceived as the customers, and customers normally go where they can get the merchandise they desire.

Because higher education is considered merchandise, students and parents are choosing colleges and universities based on competitive degree programs and the cost of such programs. Department chairs who fail to keep abreast of the trends and new developments in their respective major programs jeopardize the existence of their programs. Too many low-enrollment classes are often perceived by the average college/university administrator as signs of poor departmental planning and a good reason to discontinue a seemingly nonproductive major program. At the base of these decisions is the cost of higher education and the shrinking dollar. Wherever cuts can be made, there are dollars saved. It should be understood that administrators who are responsible for managing the money in a college or university do not think like faculty members when it comes to budgeting the dollar. Therefore, the department chair and her/his faculty must do regular feasibility studies and develop ways to survive. Competitive curricula, effective professors, and students as active customers to ensure program survival.

Second, the department chair must take the lead in assessing and updating programs. There must be a routine schedule for reviewing each major program in terms of relevancy, the number of students majoring in the program, and the number of students graduating from it. For accrediting agencies, program assessment is important. Effective assessment of programs will reveal the strengths and weaknesses in them and should lead a department to make the necessary adjustments in the curriculum. Assessment results are quickly becoming a primary tool for determining funding by some state and federal education departments. Programs which have documented data to prove that students enrolled in the programs are learning are likely to be funded. In some instances, various granting agencies are concerned about program assessment. Hence, a department chair must lead the department in developing some assessment instruments which will accurately measure student learning and program effectiveness.

Third, the department chair must understand that quality department programs cannot be built without outstanding and effective professors. Competent professors deliver competent and outstanding courses of instruction. Not only must the chair take
responsibility for recruiting strong faculty members; but, once they are hired, it is the chair's responsibility to review and evaluate them on a regular basis in order to maintain faculty accountability. Evaluations validate or invalidate faculty preparation and effectiveness in the classroom. Peer evaluations and student evaluations are also important in this process. When I left the English Department as chair and became the Dean of the School of Humanities, ninety percent of the faculty in the English Department had terminal degrees, as opposed to fifty percent when I began as chair. In the area of professional productivity in the form of publications and papers pre-

sented at discipline-related conferences, there was a significant increase in the number of faculty actively involved in publishing in referred journals and presenting papers at conferences.

It is the department chair who is left with the primary responsibility of keeping all faculty in her department accountable and aware of the fact that faculty are responsible for delivering a good product to the students, who are our customers. Without debate, faculty must show up for their classes and, once there, teach effective lessons. What is taught should be in line with historical and current scholarship in the discipline. The chair, however, must always be mindful of not crossing the line of demarcation between curriculum accountability and academic freedom. In the mission statement at Lincoln University, it is stated that faculty must be free to "teach honestly, and without fear of censure, what humankind has painfully and persistently learned about the environment and people." I would think that this should be the case at every college and university. The freedom of professors to teach honestly the truths of their discipline and lead students in the comprehension and evaluation of these truths must never be threatened by a department chair. Department chairs must protect this freedom. On the other hand, when evaluation suggests that a professor is not using time in the classroom for this purpose, the chairperson is justified in bringing this to her or his attention. I can recall several occasions when I had to confront a senior professor whose students complained that the class hour was being used to engage them in campus politics. When such issues are not addressed, students are deprived of the product for which they and their parents are paying valuable dollars.

Fourth, the department chair is the chief representative of the department and is, therefore, the primary person who articulates the policies and procedures of the department. However, an efficient chair knows that she cannot be available on the hour for every query because, aside from departmental responsibilities and teaching responsibilities, there are many extra-departmental responsibilities. I can remember when I managed the department, served as the Humanities Division Head, taught three classes, chaired the Promotions, Tenure, and Severance Committee, and advised the majority of the English majors for the duration of the academic year. Therefore, training well-informed staff and learning how to delegate authority to competent faculty members were important strategies that allowed very important to train at least one faculty member to manage the department in my absence. I also created various directorships, e.g. Director of Freshman Composition, Coordinator of the World Literature Program, and Director of the Writing-Across-the-Curriculum Program. Although these positions were non–contractural within the University, faculty were rewarded by the experience and the opportunity to enhance their curriculum vitae. For the future of a department, there should be trained faculty who could very easily move into the chairpersonship. Aside from faculty, the secretary is a very important person in the department. Usually, when one enters the office, the first person she or he encounters is the secretary. A secretary who understands department policies and procedures and has good human relations skills is an asset to the department. Many students opt for less desirable major programs or transfer to other schools because of inefficient departments. Thus, I found these to be effective strategies in increasing or maintaining student retention.

Fifth, an effective department chair is a faculty development officer. The chair must be sensitive to individual faculty development needs, both senior and junior faculty. Earlier, I mentioned the nearly fifty percent increase in English Department faculty with terminal degrees when I left the chairpersonship after twenty-three years. This increase was largely due to my commitment to recruiting the best available faculty members and my willingness to encourage junior faculty members who did not have the terminal degree to enter a doctoral program. In one case, I had a faculty member who just needed to finish her dissertation, and, in another case, the faculty member needed to get the terminal degree. In each case, the faculty member was valuable to the department, but, without the doctorate, each would lose her position. In each case, the professor took the necessary steps to get the terminal degree.

The desk of the chairperson is a receptacle for numerous opportunities that should be shared with the faculty. A good development strategy is what I call a three-year plan which must be completed by each new faculty member at the time of hire. In the plan, the faculty member outlines her or his goals and objectives over the first three years, in the areas of teaching, scholarship, and service. The chairperson can use this plan annually to monitor the faculty member's development.

Finally, the department chair must set the standards by which students, the customers perceive the product, achieve an education. However, this perception will be affected by faculty perceptions and inconsistency. Where there are differences between professors, in terms of teaching methods, there should be a common ground upon which all can meet. For example, in an English Department, one of the most difficult areas is faculty consensus on a definition of letter grades and what one should expect in a quality composition. Students tend to capitalize on the lack of consensus among faculty. The department chair has to recognize the various pedagogical differences among faculty and seek to bring faculty together on some point of agreement on the skills that the department wishes to have students master. Likewise, there needs to be clear and consistent communication of departmental standards to students. Generally, students rush to register for what they consider the "easy" professors. The department chair should make it her business to review end-of-semester faculty grades and compare them from semester to semester with all grades assigned in the department as a means of checking for the possibility of grade inflation. If students are going to have a healthy respect for academic excellence, the chair must communicate to faculty and students the high priority placed on class attendance, completion of assignments, and participation in the education process. These priorities are compromised when faculty relax departmental standards, and the department chair who ignores such faculty behavior compromises the educational process. One of my objectives, when I was a chair, was to develop uniform policies that promote academic excellence.

The procedural responsibilities of the department chair are understandably time consuming. But, the one area that I found most overwhelming was balancing my departmental responsibilities with my teaching responsibilities. I was required to teach three classes per semester in addition to all of the other responsibilities – even in a department with nine to twelve faculty members (including part-time and full-time faculty) and four major programs. I often found myself thinking of strategies to ease the situation, e.g. scheduling myself for not more than two preparations. I learned early that I could not use my office time for class preparation time. Office time was used to meet with students and faculty, as well as a multiplicity of other concerns. My evenings at home were spent on class preparations and grading student papers, along with finishing department memoranda.

The hours were long, and sleep became a luxury. Planning a teaching roster that accommodates other responsibilities, teaching at times which allow for productive office hours, and requiring conferences by appointment are some of the ways to effectuate balance. While department chairs would like to be available for everyone all of the time, this is impossible without some careful planning. A lot of time can be wasted on unplanned visits by faculty and students. As often as possible, every meeting/conference should have an agenda, or meetings can go on seemingly forever.

Perhaps, the greatest dilemma results from being a faculty member and a chair at the same time, especially when duty calls for decisive action, which may not be accepted by colleagues. A typical example is when a non-productive faculty member is applying for tenure and/or a promotion. If the chair could write a letter based on the faculty member's charm and helpfulness in the department, and ignore the person's lack of preparation and effectiveness in the classroom, writing a letter of recommendation would be less difficult and friendships would not be threatened. Unfortunately, the department chair has to understand that her job is not to win popularity contests, but rather, to maintain program accountability and faculty accountability in the classroom. On the other hand, a department chair will have those moments when she will differ with administrative directives which compromise faculty and will feel close kinship with colleagues. At these times, the department chair's first responsibility is to stand for the integrity of department programs and should not get caught up in group politics. Instead, she should find a way to communicate her differences based on sound reasoning, which will earn her the respect of colleagues and administration.

Coupled with the mastery of department responsibilities is learning to deal with human differences. Good human relations skills are important, for there is always one impossible faculty member – one who makes faculty meetings dreadful and one who never agrees with anybody or anything. As the leader, the department chair can either be the buffer or the catalyst of difficulties and of change. Throughout my tenure as chair, I encountered many difficult department meetings. Oftentimes, when I would have appreciated some support from faculty who knew that their colleague or colleagues were unreasonable, faculty just expected me alone to deal with the problem. The department chair, then, must understand that she will often have to take the heat for the faculty and work to preserve departmental peace and morale. The department chair who has poor human relations skills and feels strongly that she must respond to every unjust remark compromises her integrity and is rarely, if ever, truly respected as a leader. Truthfully speaking, what I disliked most about chairing my department were those moments in departmental meetings when a colleague or colleagues chose to be inhumanely disagreeable.

Finally, chairing an academic department can be used as a stepping stone to higher administrative positions. While the position is not purely administrative and most department chairs are considered faculty with administrative responsibilities, the administrative responsibilities – in the areas of office management, program planning and budget management – are similar to those responsibilities in top administrative positions. As the Dean of the School of Humanities, I find that what I learned as a department chair enhances my abilities in the new position. Those skills are invaluable to me now, as I try daily to make a significant difference in the quality of education offered to students at Lincoln University.

Chapter 4

Wading in the Water: Negotiating the Tenure Process

The Slippery Slope of Student Evaluations for Black Women Faculty

Beverly A. Davis

Abstract

The paper explores how factors, outside of a teacher's competence, can influence student evaluations. In particular, the university's context, reflective of the white male majority, contributes to cultural expectations that may be incompatible with those of Black women faculty. The values, beliefs, and standards of the dominant group prevail, which can contribute to unequal support and misperceptions of Black women faculty. Students are influenced by the school's culture, which can encourage students' discomfort and disjunctions with Black women faculty. Given the subjective nature of students' evaluations, these inequities can contribute to unfavorable evaluations for Black women faculty. Recommendations for addressing the proper use of student evaluations are provided.

Excellence is proclaimed the only criteria for tenure. Usually this standard has been applied to three areas of faculty responsibility: teaching, service, and scholarship. It is assumed that there are credible ways of documenting and justifying the evaluations of these faculty responsibilities. For teaching, a major means of verifying a teacher's excellence has been student evaluations. According to Coren (1998), students' evaluations have been perceived as "authoritative and unappealable" (p. 203). But are they? Moreover, how might we understand this efficient and expedient source of information (Coren, 1988) for its implications in assessing the talents of Black women faculty?

Given the stature and wide acceptance of student evaluations, one might believe that they have always been part of the Academy. According to Weinbach (1988), the consumers' movement of the 1970's with its emphasis on accountability and the student movements of the 1960's for increased influence on campuses, spurred the use of student evaluations within the Academy. It is important to appreciate this context for understanding the origins of student evaluations. Developed as a means of increasing control and accountability, they are now primarily used as instruments for faculty entry into the Academy.

The 1960's were also a time when there was an increase in the number of Black faculty on predominantly white campuses. The civil rights movement became the spur for hiring more people of color within various occupations, including the Academy. Wilson (1991) and Turner and Myers (2000) credit President Johnson's Executive Order 11246, requiring all federal contractors to embrace affirmative action, as helping to increase the number of Black faculty at white universities from zero to 2%. Moreover, Wilson (1991) asserts that the slow down of federal enforcement of affirmative action has resulted in reducing the rate of hiring Black faculty so that, today, the percentage of Black faculty is still disproportionately lower than our percentages in the overall population (Turner & Myers, 2000).

Thus, this instrument of accountability, the student evaluation, is being used to determine, if not exclude further, the number of Black faculty on campuses today. There is an assumption that students perceive all faculty, outside of their teaching competence, as equals. Therefore, the faculty's gender and race are neutral variables with no or little influence on a student's perceptions. It is my hope to explore how 1) students' perceptions are affected by contextual factors that can be linked to the race and gender of the instructor and 2) student evaluations, therefore, should be used with an understanding of these contextual realities.

What do student evaluations measure?

There is much evidence to suggest that the student's comfort with the material and the professor's style of teaching are the primary determinants of a student's evaluations (Centra, 1993). Hepworth and Oviatt (1985) reported one study that demonstrated the higher the student's anxiety level about the course, the more likely students were to give an adverse rating. Further, the same authors reported on several studies which noted that there was a direct correlation between the expected grade and the favorability of a student's evaluation (Hepworth & Oviatt, 1985). Another study found that if students were interested in the subject or took the course as an elective, they were more likely to give a higher rating to the instructor (Centra, 1993; Hepworth & Oviatt, 1985). Indeed Hepworth and Oviatt (1985) found in one study that 79% of the variance in students' evaluations could be explained by "how much did the instructor's way of teaching help you to learn?" In sum, student evaluations measure 1) the student's comfort with learning the material, and 2) the professor's communication skills (Weinbach, 1988).

With regard to the student's learning, one may argue that student evaluations should reflect how students learn in a course. However, to assume that the student's evaluation of her learning is so determinative of a professor's skills misses other important variables which are not addressed in the questions of an end-term evaluation of the instructor. For example, many student evaluations ask the students to evaluate whether the course's content was appropriate to the course. This question presumes an expertise of the students which directly contradicts their status as students (Weinbach, 1988). Furthermore, the context for the student, i.e., the student's own ability to learn the course material, is usually not included in the student's evaluation (Petchers & Chow, 1988).

Additionally, I have not seen a course evaluation which addresses the factors that may enhance or inhibit the student's learning style. For example, how might the students' comfort and commitment to learning be affected by his comfort with the professor? As one faculty in Krenzin's (1995) study noted: "Some of my students have never had a black professor, never even knew a black adult that did anything. So they look at me like, "How'd you do this?" (p. 124). Within the student evaluation process, there isn't any opportunity to identify the student's comfort with a woman of color in an authority position. In effect, the evaluations may be more applicable to the following question: how does the student's style of learning fit that of the instructor's style of teaching? Needless to say, this measurement is a less valid assessment of the instructor's expertise as an instructor. The perceived fit between a student's style of learning and the instructor's style of teaching can influence the student's evaluation of an instructor's competence. It is therefore important to understand how race and gender may influence the student's perceptions of that fit. Dissonance theory has been used by Ludwig and Meacham (1997) to help explain their findings regarding the effects of an instructor's gender and race on student's perceptions of the instructor's teaching expertise. The authors discussed a study that examined how students would rate the instructor, based on their perceived credibility of the instructor and the messages of the course content (Ludwig & Meacham, 1997). The study discovered that students were more likely to be persuaded about the course's content when they perceived the instructor to be credible. Moreover, the students tended to disregard the comments of a teacher who was perceived as only moderately credible (Ludgwig & Meacham, 1997). The authors used these findings to develop their study comparing students' reactions to instructors of different gender and race teaching controversial course content. White male instructors were assumed to have high credibility and women and people of color instructors were assumed to be of moderate credibility. Although they did not find that women and people of color instructors were rated lower, they did find that the same course content taught by white males was perceived as more controversial when taught by women and black faculty (Ludwig & Meacham, 1997). The latter finding is particularly relevant since black faculty are usually assigned course content addressing sociocultural issues which may challenge the perceived self-images and concepts of students about issues of race and gender (Turner & Myers, 2000). As one African-American female faculty member stated in Turner & Myer's (2000) study: "Regarding interaction with students, there's a different expectation for us when we walk in as a minority; they automatically assume that we know less than our colleagues in the same department . . . They challenge females more . . . So, I wear dark, tailored suits and I am very well prepared. They don't hire us unless we're prepared anyway but students think we are here because of our color" (p. 110).

Students' comfort level is also related to their interpretations of faculty behavior. To the degree that students' cultural contexts are congruent with that of the faculty member, there is the potential for greater comfort and confidence in the instructor. For example, Weinbach (1988) notes that faculty are aware of how students can be manipulated to provide higher evaluations. He writes about various strategies that faculty can use to boost their student ratings: avoid confrontations with students; provide higher grades; and by relating to the students on a first name basis, sending the message "I'm great; you're great." Further, he adds that in my discipline, where empathy is a required characteristic for effective work, students can attribute effective communications to the degree that the instructor is perceived as warm and in agreement with their attitudes (Weinbach, 1988). When these behavioral expectations become the unstated norms for faculty behavior, they can be particularly detrimental for the faculty member whom the students have interpreted does not assume these behaviors. Differences heighten what Coren (1998) refers to as the halo effect. To the degree that a bad or good trait is associated with the person, that evaluation becomes a global assessment of that person as "good" or "bad."

The Academy's Culture

In sum, student evaluations must be understood for what they can and cannot reveal about an instructor's teaching competence. Moreover, the evaluations cannot be accurately understood without attending to the organizational context. Although the previously cited studies are more exploratory than causative in their explanations about student evaluations, the variety of the findings indicate that student evaluations are not absolute indicators of a teacher's competence and must be understood in the context of the university, department, instructors, and students.

At minimum, the organizational culture must be identified and understood. In particular, it is important to understand whose values and norms are being reflected in that culture. Since most universities, outside of the historically Black colleges, are white male dominated, it should be no surprise that their values and norms predominate. Within this context, how are the values and norms of other groups accepted? What are the stated and unstated expectations of student and faculty roles within that institution? For example, what does it mean to students if a Black faculty member does not adopt the first- name-basis norm of her white counterparts? The significance of student evaluations needs to be examined within these culture and political realities order to interpret them accurately.

Another important dimension of these politics is the hiring and re-tention of black faculty. A number of studies (see, for example, Council on Social Work Education, 1974; Davis, 1985; Wilson, 1988; Sandler, 1991; Wilson, 1991; Turner & Myers, 2000) point to the universities' continued resistance to accepting, let alone, embrac-ing women and people of color faculty in university life. Outside of traditionally Black colleges, the limited numbers of African-American faculty create additional burdens for us.

When there is only one, or a very small number of black faculty members in a given institution, the burdens of institutional and indi-vidual racism weigh heavily. The psychological safety associated with numbers is not available to persons who labor in such situations. The usual protective network of sympathetic senior faculty also does not exist. Demands on black faculty time and presence escalate. In the absence of a support group operating under these same circum-stances, frustrations understandably mount. Black faculty members are subjected to the aggravating aspects of the academic milieu with-out enjoying some of its compensating benefits (Harvey & Scott-Jones in Jackson, 1991, p. 125).

The Academy's assertion of excellence (rarely defined or defined to support the status quo) as its only standards for tenure, reinforces a blindness to the presence of these inequitable burdens. At the same time, this faith in the meritocracy allows the Academy to avoid ad-dressing its own resistance to giving importance to the potency of ra-cism and sexism within its walls. Therefore, these issues are rarely examined, let alone documented, for their influence on the perceptions of Black women faculty's work (Anderson, 1988; Jackson, 1991; Turner & Myers, 2000). Moreover, this very same political context informs the measurements used to evaluate faculty, measurements based on an erroneous assumption that the context is equal and fair for all faculty. That is why the student is not challenged to examine any contextual issues that may undermine a fair and constructive evaluation of the instructor.

Moreover, a background of "Global competition, private interests and a history of exclusion in higher education combine to fuel the fires of contention within higher education today" (Turner & Myers, 2000,

p. 16). Keim and Erickson (1998) add: "Women in academia are fewer in higher ranks than men, have been less likely than men to achieve high levels of success and have been more likely to report facing numerous barriers and unequal treatment throughout the tenure and promotion process." In a survey of women academics, the stressors named were "time pressures, lack of adequate feedback and recognition, unrealistic expectations, lack of resources, and an imbalance of work and personal roles (p. 61)." For black women faculty, the confluence of race and gender combine to create significant points of disjunction, from limited social opportunities, to becoming better acquainted with senior faculty, to lack of collaboration on research, and exploration and development of their own ideas present serious barriers to their ascendancy in the academy (Krenzin, 1995). In effect, the academy is a closed system that demands acceptance of its interpretive framework of excellence for membership (Council on Social Work Education, 1974).

Strategies for a balanced use of student evaluations

One of the most important decisions about the use of student evaluations is whether their purpose is formative or summative. Formative evaluations are designed to help the instructor improve her performance and summative evaluations are used to document achievements, so clarity about their function is critical (Centra, 1993). It is most unfair to give the impression to students that the evaluations are used to help the professor improve when the purpose is part of the tenure decision process. The latter reason requires that the students be so informed so that they may use their power constructively. It is important that students appreciate the responsibility that accompanies this application of their power. Also, given the importance placed on their evaluations, students must learn about the differences between constructive and unfair feedback. Additionally, the teaching standards need to be predefined, so that students know what are the indicators for their evaluation decisions (Centra, 1993).

Further, since evaluations have different functions, their format should reflect those differences. Formative evaluations need to be designed so that they elicit constructive feedback that an instructor can use to improve her performance. Centra (1993) mentions four criteria that must be addressed for formative evaluations:

1) the evaluations provide new knowledge;

2) the information is useful;

3) the information indicates how the instructor may change; and,

4) the information is provided in a manner that motivates the instructor to change.

The student context also needs to be included (Centra, 1993). Questions about the student's own efforts and learning development in the course are helpful in identifying the student's context for taking the course. For example, to what degree did the student prepare for the course and what did the reading and writing assignments require from her? What was her understanding of the purpose of the course before and after taking it?

Centra (1993) offers guidelines for how student evaluations can be used in the promotion and tenure process. He states that 1) for each course, there should be a series of evaluations; 2) there should be sufficient numbers of students in each class so that the results are not skewed by two or three students; 3) there should be evaluations from different courses, taught by the instructor; 4) the course's characteristics should be understood as an important context, through which to interpret students' responses (examples given are teaching methods, class size, difficulty of the course material); 5) we should pay particular attention to the overall evaluation of a teacher's performance rather than each item, as an effective teacher may not score high on every dimension; and 6) there should be a standardized procedure for administering the evaluations.

Although these measures will not eliminate all biases, they can contribute to the identification of teaching patterns. But the instructor needs to be involved in making sense of these patterns. Therefore, statements from the instructor about the experience of the class should also be included. She can identify class patterns that form the backdrop for the student's comments. This inclusion also provides an opportunity for the instructor to be reflective about her own work.

In summary, a fair use of student evaluations means that the Academy must first understand its own organizational culture and particularly how this culture contributes to its teaching standards. All faculty members' values and norms need to be considered in order to justify the standards developed. Also, the primary purpose of the evaluations - formative or summative - must be clear so that both the standards and the purpose of the evaluations may be clearly interpreted for the faculty and students. Additionally, there should be a component that requires students' self-reflections about their motivation for taking the course and their own understanding of their participation in the course. Not only do these questions help students to understand their own learning process, but also the questions can contribute to understanding the student's self-interest and investment in the course.

Student evaluations in their place

Given the risks connected to student evaluations, it is important that they are balanced with other evidence of a faculty member's teaching. Expediency and efficiency ought not to be the primary motives for relying only on student evaluations as a means of judging a faculty member's teaching. The development of a teaching portfolio, for example, can be an important opportunity for an instructor to reflect on her teaching and to develop ways of enriching her teaching skills over time. By so directing our attention to an ongoing portfolio, we can keep our focus on teaching.

We are all where we are today because of an inspired teacher, someone who captured our imagination . . . And to me, this is almost a sacred art - stirring inspiration and the potential of another life (Boyer, 1993, p. 14).

References

Anderson, T. "Black encounter of racism and elitism in white academe: A critique of the system." *Journal of Black Studies* 18 (1988): 259-272.
Boyer, E. "Excellence and equity." *Black issues in Higher Education*, 10 (1993): 11-15.

Centra, J. *Reflective Faculty Evaluation: Enhancing teaching and Determining faculty effectiveness*. San Francisco: Jossey-Bass Publishers, 1993.

Chism, M. and Satcher, J. "African American students' perceptions toward faculty at historically Black colleges." *College Student Journal* 32 (1998): 315-320.

Coren, S. "Student evaluations of an instructor's racism and sexism: Truth or expedience?" *Ethics and Behavior* 8 (1998): 201-213.

Darden, J., Kamel, S. & A. Jacobs. "Black faculty in predominantly white U.S. institutions of higher education: The influence of Black student enrollment." *Equity and Excellence in Education* 31 (1998): 6-18.

Davis, L. "Black and white social work faculty: Perceptions of respect, satisfaction and job permanence." *Journal of Sociology and Social Welfare* 12 (1985): 79-84.

Davis, L., P. Freeman, L. Carter, and R. Cartwright. "Black faculty in predominantly white schools of social work: A qualitative assessment." *Journal of Education for Social Work* 19 (1983): 15 - 23.

Exum, W. "Climbing the crystal stair: Values, affirmative action and minority faculty." *Social Problems* 30 (1983): 383-399.

Hepworth, D. and Oviatt, B. "Using student course evaluations: Findings, issues and recommendations." *Journal of Social Work Education* 21 (1985): 105-112.

Jackson, K. "Factors associated with alienation among Black faculty." Research in Race and Ethnic Relations 6 (1991): 123 - 144.

Keim, J. and Erickson, C. "Women in Academia: Work-related stressors." *Equity and Excellence in Education* 31 (1998): 61-67.

Krenzin, J. "Factors influencing the retention of Black faculty on predominantly white campuses." *Research in Race and Ethnic Relations* 8 (1995): 115-138.

Kobrak, P. "Black student retention in predominantly white regional universities: The politics of faculty involvement." *Journal of Negro Education* 61 (1992): 509-530.

Ludwig, J. and Meacham, J. "Teaching controversial courses: Student Evaluations of instructors and content." *Educational Research Quarterly* 21 (1997): 27-38.

Petchers, M. and Chow, J. "Sources of variation in students' evaluation of instructors in a graduate social work program." *Journal of Social Work Education* 1 (1988): 35-42.

Sandler, B. "Women faculty at work in the classroom and why it still hurts to be a woman in labor." *Communication Education* 40 (1991): 60-66.

Turner, C. and Myers, S. *Faculty of Color in Academe: Bittersweet Success.* Boston: Allyn and Bacon, 2000.

Weinbach, R. "Manipulations of student evaluations: No laughing matter." *Journal of Social Work Education* 24 (1988): 27-34.

Wilson, R. "Developing leadership: Blacks in graduate and professional schools." *Journal of Black Studies* 19 (1988): 163-173.

Negotiating the Tenure Process

Julie E. Stokes

Abstract

My goal is to provide a step-by-step description of some of the numerous challenges faced by an African American woman negotiating the tenure process. I have identified some of the written and unwritten codes of conduct that appear to often hinder our efforts to be successful, particularly in predominantly Anglo institutions of higher learning. I believe that by openly discussing some of my challenges in meeting the requirements for tenure at an institution of higher learning which recognizes teaching and scholarly activities as the most important enterprises one needs to be successful, that other women of color can identify with the information I have outlined and use it to achieve greater success by not being aware of these possible pitfalls.

Understanding the Cultural Codes of the Academic Institution

There is an overwhelming sense of confusion at the start of the tenure process. One of the first lessons one learns when beginning her journey toward tenure is that upon entering an academic institution, she can negotiate her position within the tenure process. There are various levels of entry into the academic hierarchy. Generally, it is my understanding that new recruits start at the assistant professor level. I came to find out, however, that entering into a contract, numerous options are open and available. For example, one can negotiate whether she will be assigned to a single department or to a joint appointment in more than one academic department. One can also negotiate entry level; assistant professor, associate professor, of even in rare cases, full professor standing. Additionally, one can negotiate level of pay, as each academic level has a number of pay scale levels (e.g., A, B, C, D) and steps (e.g., 1, 2, 3, 4,) attached to the position. One can also negotiate her teaching load, requesting a reduced teaching load the first year, so as to allow her as a new recruit to establish a stable research agenda and grow accustomed to the culture of the institution.

A second area where negotiation can make a difference between success and failure within the tenure process is with regard to available resources, once a contract has been entered into. For example, will the new recruit be provided office space, a computer, with up-to-date software, a telephone, and needed supplies to be successful. Though these seem reasonable assumptions, they cannot simply be taken for granted. Therefore, one should always ask for these things up front.

When one is negotiating tenure, there must be a keen awareness and understanding of the institution's Written Codes. All formal institutional structures generally have a set of written guidelines (cultural codes) by which they operate. These are often identified as Standard Operating Procedures. Therefore, one of the first tasks that is reasonable to undertake is to review these documents which are usually made available upon hire. The institutional regulations and standards outline what is required in order to move toward tenure. The areas that are often considered are organized in a rubric from most important to least and generally these include teaching, research, and service. Different institutions place varying levels of importance on various activities, so talk to others and find out where the institution you are involve in stands on the importance of any area one must achieve in order to obtain tenure. Find out, for example, if teaching carries more weight or if the institution is more focused on research.

Talking with others in the institutional setting was one of the most difficult tasks I faced. There were a number of factors that hindered my efforts. For example, as a woman of color, I often perceived a linguistic barrier between myself and others. This barrier appeared to be reflected in my cultural expressions which others did not understand. For example, the fact that I see myself as assertive while others within academia saw me as aggressive left me feeling unsure about the level of openness I could and should exhibit. Then there was the challenge of framing of questions in a manner most readily understandable to my colleagues. Due to my lack of experience and background with academia, it often felt much more comfortable to sit and listen rather than to contribute to discussions taking place. In fact, I was often instructed not to be to open and thus not make errors in statements I made if I wanted to be successful in achieving tenure. The approach of remaining silent possibly works against me, as it is often perceived as a lack of involvement with regard to the activities for which I was responsible.

Various institutions place emphasis on certain aspects of employment responsibilities. Thus, negotiation of role requirements can lead to role strain. One automatically assumes the role of a teacher upon entering an academic institution. Yet, the competing dictates of the role are not always outlined. For example, in addition to preparing new courses; selecting texts, preparing course material, developing exams, developing assignments, one has to respond to the character of the class once it has begun. Thus, one needs to have effective leadership skills, presentation skills, negotiating skills, and sometimes even counseling skills in order to be successful with students.

Student evaluations of teaching enter into the tenure and promotion process, putting additional strain on the new professor in her quest for tenure. Students' sentiments can often affect a faculty member's success. Students indicate whether or not they perceive the instructor as being well-prepared. Yet, students have absolutely no practical experience in regard to what it takes to prepare for a class, much less the effort involved in the effective delivery of instructional material. Students also indicate if they felt the grading was fair. There are no criteria by which a student could make such an assessment, except whether or not they received the particular grade they wanted. Students respond to these types of questions and then an overall course score (usually a mean) is calculated. These course means are compared across departmental and campus-wide standards that place new and inexperienced faculty members at a disadvantage. The bottom line is if students like the faculty member's style of instruction or method of information delivery, the instructor scores well. If not, poor student evaluations are imminent and inevitable.

An additional institutional requirement often relates to research. Research requires time commitment; that is time to read, think, develop a research plan, collect and analyze information, write, review, rewrite, identify constituents interested in your product, and get published in peer review outlets. Rarely, however, is a newly-hired faculty member in a position to dedicate such time solely to research. Consequently, the new challenge that arises is how to become a productive scholar.

Moreover, how does one identify research questions that are viewed as practical and important to one's colleagues? The activities attached to becoming a successful scholar in order to achieve tenure are enormous. Therefore, there will eventually have to be sacrifices made. These sacrifices require that priorities be set so that there is enough time to attend to the requisite activities that will further one's move toward tenure. Sometimes working with others on a manuscript is an option.

The task of getting published in peer review journals is the most challenging when considering the time constraints under which one is working. There is the task of developing research around an interesting and significantly important question, according to the normative scholarly standards of one's discipline and then the time involved in conducting scholarly research activity. Once a manuscript has been completed, it is submitted to a peer review journal for publication. Take note however, it is important to identify and approach a journal editor that one feels will be interested in one's work. As a newly professional scholar, the task of identifying someone who may be interested in the work one is pursuing is truly a trial and error process.

Again, there is research and information gathering that must take place if one is to be efficient in this activity. Even so, once a prospective publisher is identified and the manuscript submitted, one has to simply wait for the review process to take its course. Perhaps the hardest part for all writers is the inevitable waiting period required to see if the manuscript is accepted for review.

If the manuscript is not accepted for review, a few questions arise: (1) should the manuscript be submitted to another journal, (2) should the manuscript be reviewed and possibly the focus modified, or (3) should the effort be abandoned altogether? Of course while one is making a decision, the tenure clock is ticking. In any case, one has to write and get published in journals that require manuscript reviews by other scholars recognized in that particular field of study.

Educational institutions, like other service-oriented organizations, require faculty to take on the role of service provider. I feel that the opportunity to be of service to students, colleagues, surrounding communities, and the institution that employed me is a tremendous honor. Still, I have had to understand the requirements of the role before undertaking the responsibility for so many categories of service. For example, there is what is identified as service to the academic institution and then there is service to the community. Service to the academic institution often includes meeting with students, serving on campus committees, participating in special campus events (e.g., conferences, seminars, workshops, etc.), to name but a few. Additionally, there is service to the community. The community can be the academic community (e.g., graduation ceremonies) or the community surrounding the academic institution (e.g., civic and social organizations). No matter which community one is serving, be cognizant of both the responsibilities of the commitment and the time necessary to be effective are imperative. Over commitment of one's time, skills, and talent can lead quickly to burnout.

Time commitments that are often spread out among numerous competing responsibilities can be extremely difficult to manage successfully. For example, family members will feel slighted or left out of one's life as greater and greater attention is given to work activities. Then, it seems as if one is not even totally effective at tasks related to work, as there is little or no time for rest and relaxation. A feeling of frustration and then stress can begin to develop. Whereupon, a lack of the ability to concentrate and focus on tasks develops and this becomes even more challenging. The feelings often can become overwhelming. So, one either re-conceptualizes the events through prayer and one's faith or considers giving in to the emotions and possibly giving up. There often is no one to speak with openly and honestly about these feelings and frustrations due to the uncertainty of how other colleagues will respond to one's concerns.

There is a constant need to recognize that as a participant in an institution of higher learning, one will assume the role of a continuing learner. Academic institutions often recognize the need to provide continued development opportunities to the faculty. This is accomplished in various ways. It may be through attending professional conferences, joining peers in special projects, gaining extra training, or taking on new and even more challenging assignments. These activities are necessary if one is going to be successful in her bid for tenure, but how much and how often remains an individual decision.

Review and evaluation are a necessary part of assessing the effectiveness of any employment. So, it is important to begin immediately preparing a portfolio related to activities. There will come a time in the tenure process where one must tell others how one has utilized her time and what she has accomplished. BE PREPARED! Document, Document, Document. It is probably helpful, as each period of instruction ends and teaching evaluations are made available that one sit down and review student comments, determine a course of action in response to student comments, and document, in writing, every decision that is being made and why. New teaching approaches used should be recorded. New or different text adoption should be addressed. Modifications made in exam methodology should be explained. What worked and what did not work must be explored. These reflections and acts of conscientiousness about every course, every student comment, every success and failure can prove invaluable as the novitiate faculty member proves scholarly prowess to a tenure committee.

Getting published remains necessary. Still, manuscripts that are still being developed can be submitted in draft form. Never offer up unsuccessful attempts at publication. It can only call into question one's ability. Always provide documentation of the peer review process. And in the immortal words of Winston Churchill, "Never give up. Never give up. Never give up."

The organization of materials is just as important as what is included in the documents. Once all information has been gathered together, place it in binders in a neat and organized fashion. Separate information into the categories provided by the academic institution. One should offer supporting documentation for all entries. It is important to check and cross check so as to be sure there are not any inconsistencies in the documentation.

If the opportunity has arisen to participate as faculty in an institution of higher learning, then it is likely that the necessary resources are present for meeting the challenge of becoming tenured. The tenure process itself often seems straightforward. There are tasks to complete that are generally outlined. These are the academic institution's cultural codes of conduct for success. Still, less evident are the implicit dictates of the institution that will facilitate success in the tenure process. These include procedures on negotiating one's position in the academic hierarchy, pay, resources, and time allocation.

Become aware of which sacrifices one is willing to make in order to achieve tenure. There may need to be sacrifices made with regard to time spent on activities outside of the academic institution, including family and other support systems, at least temporarily. There may need to be sacrifices made with regard to one's opportunities to freely and openly express one's experiences, beliefs, and ideas. There will definitely need to be sacrifices made in regard to one's time. So, simply know which sacrifices are important to make in order to achieve tenure.

Lessons from African American Faculty Women: Practical Strategies to Securing Tenure

Sheila T. Gregory

Abstract

This paper will: 1) identify common obstacles to tenure and offer practical solutions to address them; 2) provide a checklist of essential questions you must ask to thoroughly understand the departmental culture and expectations and; 3) outline strategies African American faculty women have successfully employed to secure tenure.

According to the American Association of University Professor's (AAUP) 1940 Statement of Principles, tenure offers: (1) the freedom to teach and conduct research and (2) economic security. Tenure track faculty positions in American higher education are typically measured by the ranks of assistant, associate, and full professor. Tenure is described as an arrangement by which faculty appointments continue until retirement age, although they are subject to dismissal for adequate cause or termination due to financial exigency or change of institutional programs in higher education institutions (AAUP, 1973). Tenure is said to serve as a lifetime guarantee that professors will receive due process within the context of the academic institution, although interpretation of academic freedom and protection vary. According to the AAUP, nearly 85 percent of all American colleges and universities use the tenure system and these institutions maintain that the tenure system employs approximately 95 percent of all full-time faculty. Tenure, in all fairness, is a process of exclusion. The essence of the tenure system today is based on a process that was developed by and for an academy composed primarily of non-minority men who have not shared the same interests, needs, views, or experiences of Black women. Some institutions have also argued against tenure because of the financial obligation, but numerous scholars have suggested workable solutions such as imposing a post-tenure review process (Finkin, 1996) to increase the flexibility of institutions to hold tenured faculty accountable for performance.

At research institutions, the three most widely used indicators for tenure decisions are the number of publications, the caliber of publications, and recommendations from outside scholars (Carnegie Foundation, 1990). Most faculty publications are in the form of journal articles and the three most common techniques used for ranking professional journals are the journal's reputation, citations, and rejection rates (Seldin, 1993). Although tenure timelines vary across institutions, the national norm is achieving tenure by the sixth year. However, realistically, there are only five years at most to develop a tenure dossier since it takes at least a year, on average, for work to be published and for the tenure process to be completed. While it is not unheard of for an outstanding young assistant professor to be recognized for promotion early in the fourth or fifth year, it is not likely because institutions do not want to set a precedent. Furthermore, if the candidate fails, it could unfavorably color her chances in the future. The key is getting annual written performance appraisals so faculty are aware of the new faculty member's progress and available documentation.

This paper will: 1) identify common obstacles to tenure and offer practical solutions to address them; 2) provide a checklist of essential questions you must ask to thoroughly understand the departmental culture and expectations and; 3) outline strategies African American faculty women have successfully employed to secure tenure.

Effective mentoring of junior faculty has been shown to enhance one's success at achieving tenure (Blackwell, 1989; Gregory, 1999). Mentoring is when a person uses her own experiences and expertise to help guide the development of another through encouragement and praise, quality time, constructive criticism, intellectual discussion and debate, and a host of other professional activities. Mentors can serve as friends, career guides, information sources, and/or intellectual guides to provide advice, protection, and a genuine concern for a protégé's career progress. Blackwell (1989) found that mentoring was important because it directly influenced the number of Black and other minority students attending and graduating from colleges and universities. In fact, according to Blackwell, mentoring of minority students was one of the primary reasons cited by colleges and universities for diversifying their faculty. Gregory (1999) found that African American faculty women relied most heavily on mentoring and support because of the need for guidance, strength, and encouragement in academic settings that were often unfriendly and isolating.

Support systems were found to be most significant for academic women trying to maintain the demands of marriage, family, and career. African American faculty women who were married most often reported their spouse and children as a major source of support, while single women reported parents and friends as being the most supportive. Gregory (1999) also found that the presence of mentors was reported to enhance one's opportunity for promotion and tenure, primarily because it provided important information needed for professional competence, time management, and discipline. Effective mentors ranged broadly by gender, profession, discipline, and ethnicity, however, the majority of women faculty reported having several mentors, often simultaneously, in disciplines and professions different from their own.

Several essential questions should be asked by non-tenured faculty in order to clearly understand and accept elements of the departmental culture, and learn what responsibilities are expected of them to be successful at tenure and promotion. Schoenfield and Magnan (1994) identified five questions a faculty member needs to ask. First, who are the leaders--formal and informal--in the department and are they positive or negative toward you professionally and personally? Second, are there other responsibilities expected that you will be evaluated on which are not outlined in your appointment letter? Third, what standards must you meet in each of your years in the department? Fourth, what norms or culture in the department must you recognize and respect? And finally, what are the strengths and weaknesses of the department and among the department's faculty, staff, and students?

Whicker, Kronenfeld, and Strickland (1993) argue that junior faculty need to assess the political aspects of securing tenure. They recommend: a) examining the effects of being granted tenure in the department as a whole -- are you seen as a threat or contributor?; b) determining the effect of being granted tenure on those already tenured; c) being supportive of the chair and dean; and d) determining whether there is a need for your expertise within the institution.

Once these questions have been answered, a five to six-year professional academic plan should be developed for tenure and promotion. In addition, the plan should be reviewed and possibly revised every six months. Simply begin the process by identifying strengths and weaknesses, setting realistic objectives and goals with measurable outcomes, and evaluating progress each year.

Strategies for obtaining tenure

The best strategies for obtaining tenure can be learned from the obstacles African American faculty women have reported while trying to climb the academic ladder. Some obvious obstacles, such as lack of job mobility due to personal circumstance, family factors, race and gender, need to be recognized but are not usually within a person's control and therefore will not be discussed.

Some argue that African American and other women of color often choose to participate in time-consuming activities, such teaching and advising a proportionately greater share of undergraduate students, serving on committees, overburdening themselves with service-related activities, and publishing infrequently and primarily in non refereed, non mainstream journals. Chamberlain (1991) has argued that these types of activities reduce the scholarly productivity of faculty women and consequently hinder their career progress.

The following seven important strategies will help overcome these common pitfalls. First, as I mentioned earlier, **develop an aggressive but realistic action plan** to achieve promotion and tenure with semi-annual goals and measurable outcomes. Ask a mentor to review them and help keep you on track by providing constant feedback and assisting you in locating valuable resources. Determine your knowledge and skills and continue to hone them – including your knowledge and comfortability with scholarly, technical, communication, analysis, and synthesis information. Evaluate and know your individual beliefs, professional standards and convictions, and trust them to dictate your actions.

Second, **avoid isolation** at all costs and make sure you become well-integrated within your department and College. For example, work on developing effective relationships with colleagues, chairs, deans, and those within and outside your institution and discipline. Go out to lunch with colleagues and discuss how you can collaborate on research and grant projects. Reach out to senior faculty. Find at least one and preferably three academic mentors in your discipline-- both within and outside your institution--with whom you feel comfortable and share common interests. Meet with them regularly and welcome others with similar beliefs. Network, network, network by establishing potentially advantageous professional relationships early on with those academic leaders in your field who may likely be called upon to make recommendations for leadership positions, grants, research funds, tenure, and promotion. Use national and international conferences to hone your research and field your resume on an ongoing basis. Identify and cultivate all the resources you uncover. Maintain professional contact with graduate students through your thesis and dissertation research, and offer talented students an opportunity to publish with you. Make yourself visible in the community and build community support. Build a coalition among colleagues in and outside your department and institution. Seek out those whom you admire in your field, get them on the phone, and talk to them or write occasionally to let them know what you are doing and ask their advice. Initiate professional networks with prominent people in your field so you'll have some names to suggest for evaluation when tenure comes around.

Third, learn how to appropriately, yet firmly, **say 'no'** when you are asked to engage in unnecessary activities that will detract you from your research. While it is important to ensure that you carry your own weight and are viewed as collegial, it should be no more your responsibility than other faculty unless a reduced load is offered to you as a junior faculty member in your department. Aisenberg and Harrington (1988) wisely recommend always asking, 'what's in it for me?' before agreeing to take on more tasks.

Fourth, **discipline yourself** each summer to write and submit at least one article to a refereed journal, regardless of whether you choose to teach in the summer or take a vacation. It goes without saying that one must consistently conduct quality research and publish in scholarly, refereed journals in her field of expertise.

Fifth, **learn as quickly as possible who your friends are** and who they are not. Determine whom you can trust and whom you should avoid, and be sure to listen much more than you talk. When in academic meetings, resist comment on important issues until you know where everyone else in the room stands. In academe, and particularly at the department level, faculty members have very long memories. The moment a person comes up for promotion or tenure, everything she has ever said or done can be scrutinized.

Sixth, **try to quietly succeed whenever possible**, especially to those in your own department, so you will be viewed as a team player and not a threat to others. Publications, however, are the exception to the rule. Be sure to amass and distribute a supply of your published papers, article reprints, and citations. Also, graciously respond to the local media and become a visible advocate in your local community. Keep every letter, note, or clipping from community. Keep every letter, note, or clipping from your students, faculty, administrators, the media along with student/faculty evaluations or any other professional documents for your annual performance appraisal. Likewise, keep copies of all presentation materials, programs, papers, handouts, evaluations, and similar documents. Seventh, **keep your private, personal business to yourself** and off campus. Maintain a private, detailed record of any discrimination or harassment you've experienced and keep it at home. Finally, **constantly improve and hone your skills** by attending and actively participating in professional conferences, forums, and panels. Share your advice and skills with African American and other women and faculty of color.

Conclusion

In conclusion, African Americans today make up roughly 23 percent of the 526,324 faculty who teach at American colleges and universities. Approximately 4.8 percent of the 23 percent of full professors are African American, 2.6 percent teach at the associate level, 7.7 percent are assistant professors, and 8.1 percent teach at the instructor or lecturer level (AAUP, 1998).

It has become apparent that African American faculty women need to do all they can to accept, support, and promote other women and faculty of color, especially when it comes to securing tenure. Many often seek intellectual stimulation through participation in professional organizations and associations, both within and outside the discipline. These professional networks provide numerous advantages in obtaining a position, becoming successful, and achieving tenure and promotion. First of all, professional networks can serve as a vehicle for professional mobility by helping one access greater information regarding job opportunities. Some have emphasized the importance associations play in obtaining a professional position (Gregory, 1999). Knowing the right people and being told about the right job at the right time greatly enhances opportunity. Secondly, once a position is secured, professional networks can help affirm oneself and one's abilities, enhance one's social network, enable one to share ideas and collaborate on projects, offer peer evaluation of scholarship and intellectual stimulation, teach the proper protocols, and offer greater professional visibility. Finally, professional networks can help enhance the opportunity for promotion by sharing information on unwritten criteria for promotion and tenure, and offer letters of support, particularly if members are in the same professional discipline.

And finally, professional relationships and friendships with other academic women on and off campus are very important because they serve several purposes. First, they can assist in shaping a woman's own identity as a legitimate scholar. Second, they can collaborate and help each other develop effective research strategies. And third, they serve to alleviate the feeling of isolation common among minority and new faculty, perhaps exponentially so when one balances both identities simultaneously. Similarly, women in the Gregory study (1999) expressed the need and importance of a shared understanding, mutual respect, trust, and support among other faculty women.

References

Aisenberg, N. and M. Harrington. *Women of Academe: Outsiders in the Sacred Grove*. Amherst: University of Massachusetts Press, 1988.

American Association of University Professors. *Academic Freedom and Tenure*, 1973.

American Association of University Professors. *Statement of Principles and Interpretive Comments*. Washington, D.C.

American Association of University Professors. 1998. "The Annual Report on the Economic Status of the Profession," issues annual. *Academe* (July/August): 23 (1998).

Blackwell, J. "Mentoring: An Action Strategy for Increasing Minority Faculty." *Academe* (Sept/Oct): 8-14 (1989).

Carnegie Foundation for the Advancement of Teaching. *Identifying Comparable Institutions*. Washington, DC: John Minter Associates, 1990.

Chamberlain, M., ed., *Women in Academe: Progress and Prospects* (New York: Russell Sage Foundation, 1991).

Finkin, M. *The Case for Tenure*. Ithaca: Cornell University Press, 1996.

Gregory, S. *Black Women in the Academy: The Secrets to Success and Achievement*. Lanham, MD: University Press of America, 1999.

Schoenfield, A. C. and R. Magnan. *Mentor in a Manual: Climbing the Academic Ladder to Tenure*. Madison, WI: Atwood Publishing, 1994.

Seldin, P. "How Colleges Evaluate Professors." *AAHE Bulletin*, October 1993, 6-8:12.

Whicker, M., J, Kronenfeld, and R. Strickland. *Getting Tenure.* Newbury
Park, CA: Sage Publications, 1993.

Finding Calm Waters During the Tenure Process: A Dozen Anchors for Success

Cheryl Evans Green & Rebekah McCloud

Abstract

Most articles on Black women faculty focus on their failure to advance their careers in colleges and universities, but this paper describes twelve (12) strategies that Black females can use to be successful in obtaining tenure. These strategies are identified by the authors as a dozen anchors to calm, or at least make calmer, the turbulent waters often encountered during the tenure process. Based on the work of previous researchers who have examined the obstacles faced by women faculty and faculty of color as they attempt to achieve tenure, the paper discusses how Black female faculty can use the following dozen anchors to successfully obtain tenure. This paper contains practical and specific strategies that a Black female faculty member can proactively use to be seen as a competent, confident, and credible professional and to ensure that she will become tenured.

Even though in recent years affirmative action may have opened the doors of campuses to new Black faculty, many observers indicate that Black faculty still face a number of obstacles in establishing, maintaining, and advancing their academic careers (Singh, Robinson & Williams-Green, 1995; Wiley, 1992; Smith, 1985). Wiley (1992) noted Minority faculty are hired with the assumption that they will serve as educator, counselor, mentor, and guardian for minority students (p. 4). Black faculty are frequently expected to perform these roles in addition to dealing with the normal teaching, research, and service hurdles that all faculty face in obtaining tenure.

Some faculty of color see themselves as do-alls and their colleagues as do-littles, Wiley (1992, p. 5) indicated. To support his observations, Wiley (1992, p. 5) quoted a Black professor of literature: "I was hired to teach African American and women's literature, but there was also the expectation that a Black professor would be all things to all people, especially when it comes to representing the race." Andrews (1993) expressed similar concerns about the multiple, and sometimes conflicting, demands placed on Black faculty:

The Black professor is often called upon to serve as a mentor and counselor to African American students in an environment that is often hostile to them. The consequences of these multifaceted expectations by students are compounded by the existence of similar demands placed upon Blacks by colleagues and administrators. If we consider the fact that Blacks often also have the same expectations to meet at home, it is abundantly clear that in many cases something has to give (page 73).

Some faculty, however, must contend with more than the usual difficulties. If you're a woman, a member of an ethnic minority group, or a foreigner, the ladder to tenure may be more slippery (Schoenfeld & Magnan, 1994, p. 77). Black women are frequently depicted as facing a form of double jeopardy in the academy related to being tenured and promoted (Zunker, 1998; Lindsay, 1994; Wiley, 1992; Moses, 1989). Graves (1990) pointed out that:

From the moment a Black female accepts a faculty position at a predominately White institution, she has a different job description than does her White male or female counterpart. As a Black faculty member, she is expected to participate on every administrative committee that might possibly confront minority issues. The Black woman faculty is also expected to serve as mentor to all Blacks and, in some instances, all minority students. Finally, tenure decisions do not value or even evaluate these types of service to the institution (p. 7).

While only 500 were expected, more than 2,000 Black women faculty attended a conference at the Massachusetts Institute of Technology (MIT) in January 1994 to discuss the gains they had made in the past decade and the double jeopardy they continue to encounter as both Black and female. These women spoke of the double-binds of racism and sexism, and of the burdens of serving as mentors to Black female students when Black women faculty are so few on any particular campus.

MIT's president, Dr. Charles M. Vest, was impressed with the focus of the gathering. He characterized the conference's significance in identifying the multiple obstacles that Black women face in academe by saying: "I can't help but think that this conference is a major step in making the invisible visible," (Leatherman, 1994, p. 19). Both the pride and pain of being a Black woman in the academy are also echoed by others who state that:

At the intersection of race and gender stands women of color, torn by the lines of bias that currently divide white from nonwhite, male from female. The worlds these women negotiate demand different and often wrenching allegiances. As a result, women of color are expected to meet performance standards set for the most part by white males. Yet, their personal lives extract a loyalty to their culture that is central to acceptance by family and friends. At the same time, they must struggle with their own identity as women in a society where thinking like a woman is still considered a questionable activity. At times, they can experience pressure to choose between their racial identity and their womanhood (Carter, Pearson & Shavlik, 1987/88, p. 98).

Trying to achieve tenure often means that Black female faculty must swim in deep and dangerous waters. Finding calm, or at least calmer, waters, which allow them to swim with some degree of safety during the tenure process, is a must if Black women are to successfully navigate and negotiate the tenure process.

Women of color in the academy, particularly Black female faculty, who are pursuing tenure may profit from following the guerrilla tactics identified by Rose (1992) in her useful article, 10 tips to tenure: Guerilla tactics for women in a research university. Bishop (2000) also identified viable strategies for career advancement in the academy that she termed the thirteen commandments of survival. It is important to note that Bishop (2000) suggested that there needed to be thirteen commandments, not just ten. "Moses needed only ten commandments... but he wasn't dealing with [academia] and he wasn't a woman of color," (p. 2).

Anchors for Success

Adapting from and building on the work of both Rose (1992) and Bishop (2000), this article identifies a dozen anchors which the authors believe can assist Black female faculty to calm the waters and be seen as competent, confident, and credible professionals who can be successful in obtaining tenure.

Anchor #1: Set career goals and be clear about where tenure fits in achieving them.

According to Williams (1989), people who are making long-range career plans should have an idea of what route is most efficient and effective for reaching their goal. Know where you are going in the next three to five years. Thriving in the academy is not a simple endeavor, particularly for Black women. In fact, Verrier (1993) observed that faculty who acquire tenure-track positions in today's academic climate must prepare for what will be for some an enduring trial (p. 97). Since tenure is an up or out process, one should be prepared to move up or get out. Assess your priorities, strengths, and weaknesses and set a deliberate plan for obtaining your career goals. If tenure is an objective along the path to meeting your longer-term career goals, go for it.

Anchor #2: Cultivate a professional network, both inside and outside your department.

Develop a network with prominent colleagues and other professionals in your field, including other Black female faculty who may share your experiences of life in the academy, so that at tenure time you will have some individuals outside your institution to suggest as evaluators of your tenure portfolio. This is especially important if your college or university requires that reviewers outside your school provide formal feedback on your teaching, research, and service record when you apply for tenure. In fact, some schools ask outside reviewers to give an opinion about whether you should actually receive tenure.

If at all possible, find a mentor. If you are not able to find a mentor in your department or school, locate someone at another school to mentor you who is willing and able to meaningfully and consistently contribute to your advancement. Almost all of the research on successful women has identified the presence of role models, mentors, sponsors, or other supportive relationships as a primary factor in their career advancement of women in any field (Bishop, 2000; Rodriguez, 1996; Singh, Robinson & Williams-Green, 1995; Konrad, 1992). Informal support from any of these sources may assist a Black woman in a number of ways: augment a Black woman's competence; increase her career aspirations; enhance her self-confidence; and, provide her with varying degrees of opportunity and credibility. Bishop (2000, p.1) warned, however, that one should:

> ...be wary... of becoming so slavish in your imitation of your mentor that you become a caricature... In dealing with your mentor, you will need to walk a fine line... remaining friendly and admiring but always professional.

Some observers have indicated that few people, particularly Black women, have a single mentor. Most successful people frequently have multiple lines of support from a variety of persons who perform a range of mentoring functions at different times (Johnson, 1998; Rodriguez, 1996; Konrad, 1992; Kanter, 1977). Women are cautioned to avoid what has been termed mentor mania and are advised that several helping relationships might need to be substituted for a mentor (Fury, 1979), rather than searching in vain for the all-purpose mentor.

Potential sources of effective and useful mentoring-like guidance and support are relationships with superiors, peers, and even clerical staff, both inside and outside of the department. Find people among your work groups who can serve as coaches or cheerleaders who provide realistic and timely encouragement when the tenure waters "get rough, and even rougher," or "silent sponsors" in administration who admire you and with whom you can build a mutually beneficial alliance. These individuals need to be people who will support and promote your work. They need to be people who know how things really work when it comes to getting tenure in your department and school. They need to be willing to honestly and openly share this information because they have a genuine investment in your success.

Anchor #3: Promote your work by becoming your own public relations person.

Make sure that you keep on hand an ample supply of reprints of your publications. Circulate these reprints to your colleagues and other academics at your school and other institutions that have similar research interests. Make sure you get mentioned, on a regular basis, in the faculty newsletter and other printed or electronic resources on your campus that provide information about faculty members' research and service activities. Making your colleagues aware of your contributions to the school and community is critically important for Black women, whose work, especially service contributions, can often be invisible to others because they may assume that service is just normally woman's work.

Anchor #4: Be sure that your teaching is at least adequate.

If there are problems with your teaching, particularly if your student evaluations contain low ratings of your teaching performance, consult your campus faculty development center. In fact, if your teaching is acceptable, you may still want to use the faculty development center to enhance, improve, and enrich your teaching. Few people, no matter what their talents and abilities may be, are born good teachers. Good teachers usually learn to be good teachers. Often development centers can provide faculty with information and other materials (e.g., model syllabi; critiques of videotaped lectures; examples of effective course evaluation strategies; teaching tips for managing the classroom environment) to significantly improve their teaching.

In addition to the faculty development center, a number of publications are very useful guides for teaching excellence. For example, Pregent (1994) in *Charting your course* describes systemic and systematic approaches to prepare to do good teaching. Weimer & Neff (1990) offer creative guidelines for effective course planning, teaching, and evaluation. Weimer, & Kerns (1988) even provide forms and activities that can be used to get instructional feedback from students that can be used to improve one's teaching. Lastly, Lowman (1984), in *Mastering the techniques of teaching*, provides instruction on how to present exciting lectures, conduct stimulating discussions, and interact with students to promote motivation, critical thinking, and independent learning.

Anchor #5: Learn to manage your time, especially how to ration your service activities.

The notion that time is on your side is a faulty assumption. In fact, time is your enemy. Learn to manage it or it will manage you. Do not overload yourself with service. Service, although an essential component of faculty and administrative life, does not count for much in the tenure process. However, service is an integral component of the socialization of people of color. Often admonished to lift as you climb, Black women are especially susceptible to overloading themselves. Select one or two service projects to focus on. Accept any high-profile committee assignment. Say no to everything else. Women must evaluate carefully the tasks at which they work hard, advised Smith (1985, p. 16).

Anchor #6: Establish a comprehensive employment file.

Include letters of recommendation and commendation from supervisors and colleagues in your file. Consider putting in the file positive notes from students about the quality of your teaching, statements from others noting helpful advisement that you provided, and information concerning your contributions to student-related service activities. Also, do not forget to place in the file letters received from people in the community and/or other campuses that praise your professional contributions or service work. Be sure to document all of your presentations, publications, lectures, workshops, creative projects, and grant-writing endeavors. This information will later become the basis of your vitae and tenure portfolio. You need to keep copies of your annual reviews. Also keep a private, detailed record of any racial discrimination or sexual harassment that you have experienced. This documentation may come in handy if you are turned down for tenure. If you are turned down for tenure and you believe that the decision was unjust, consider filing a grievance. Or face the fact that you may find a better fit elsewhere in a position at another college or university.

Anchor #7: Conduct a frank, third-year review and appraisal of your progress toward tenure.

If not required by your department or school, request that you receive an annual formal review of the progress that you are making toward achieving tenure. This can be especially important for women of color since they are often newer arrivals on the academic scene and their research and service interest may be unfamiliar to more traditional faculty. Try to ensure that this appraisal is done by or in consultation with tenured department members, or their designated committee. The purpose of the appraisal should be to provide you with assistance and counseling to aid you to qualify for tenure. It usually contains an overall rating of other faculty members perceptions of your progress, ranking you either above, at, or below expectation in progressing toward tenure. Although such appraisals are normally not binding in an institution, an appraisal is especially important in your third year because it gives you a midpoint assessment of where others in your department believe you stand related to earning tenure.

Anchor #8: Use criticism to your advantage.

Consider criticism corrective feedback that you can decide to either use or not use to make changes in your behavior. As Bishop (2000) notes, in her discussion of career success strategies: "Weight the criticism objectively, consider its merit, and take steps to correct your shortcomings. If you can't correct them all, you at least get (an) A for effort (p. 3)." However, you must react in writing to any negative annual evaluation immediately. State your case explicitly in your employment file. If the annual tenure appraisals of your progress toward tenure have been consistently negative, start looking for another job.

Anchor #9: Bet on yourself.

Allen (1997) has given career advice to corporate women that also seems applicable to Black female faculty. Women seeking to advance in their professions are urged by Allen to have confidence in their abilities and skills to meet their goals:

> You know you better than anyone else. So if you think that you can, do it! If you want to, you can. You control your own drive, discipline, and desire. Bet on yourself. You'll find when you do, others will bet on you too. Keep your eye on the clock. You know better than anyone else when your growth has slowed. Try to stay

with your game plan, but stay willing to take advantage of unexpected opportunity. Your career clock is important because you need to have time to run the plays you need to win (p. 49).

Anchor #10: Maintain loving relationships with family and friends.

A number of observers indicate that the family and friends of people of color, most notably Black women faculty, are invaluable resources in providing much of the nonprofessional support required for career advancement (Bishop, 2000; Rodriguez, 1996; Konrad, 1992; Wiley, 1992). Just as it may take a village to raise a child, it often takes a village of family and friends to support a Black woman as she attempts to advance her career. Such support may be information and/or advice, which is perceived to have beneficial social, psychological, and affective value for the recipient. This circle of caring and supportive relationships may also include ancestors that Black women honor. As Sellner (1990) noted in *Mentoring: The ministry of spiritual kinship*:

> Each of us contains within our fragile vessels of skin and bones and cells this inheritance of soul. We are links between the ages, containing past and present expectations, sacred memories and future promise. Only when we recognize that we are heirs can we truly be pioneers (p. 145).

Anchor #11: Keep your soul alive.

It is extremely important for Black women to stay grounded. In the last decade, much has been written about spirituality and its impact on job performance. Zen, Yoga, various forms of meditation, and spiritual expression have been touted as one of the four components necessary for total wellness (proper nutrition, exercise, and sleep are the other three). According to Southern (1996), for many African American women, spirituality has been a main source of sustenance behind the quantum leaps they have made in predominately white colleges and universities (p. 25). Keep your soul alive. Find ways to engage in activities that tend to the soul, which is activities that are relaxing, refreshing, and renewing.   Arrien (1993) advised women to appreciate themselves.

> Some Shamanic traditions in parts of Africa and the Oceanic societies attend to health and well-being through what is called cradling work, a four-part practice in staying connected to the good, true, and beautiful aspects of one's nature. In cradling work, we lie on our backs and place both hands over our hearts (in many cultures hands symbolize healing). Silently, we acknowledge the character qualities that we appreciate about ourselves, we acknowledge our strengths, we acknowledge the contributions that have been made and continue to be made, and we acknowledge the love given and received (pp. 61-62).

Anchor #12:   Above all else remember: YOU ARE NOT YOUR JOB!

Your worth as a person should not rest on your department's evaluation of you. Be positive about yourself as a leader. Never forget that you would not have gotten as far as you have if you did not have talents and abilities. Bennis (1983) noted that leaders know their own worth; they have positive self regard (p.64). Take stock of yourself, your skills, and your accomplishments.

In summary, Black, female faculty need to develop success and survival strategies:

> Be active and energetic on your own behalf. Develop a strategy that will guide your progress over the next five years. Seek information, advice and assistance, particularly about promotion-and-tenure criteria at your institution. Keep careful records of your activities. Develop your own networks. Above all, don't turn and run, withdraw into apathy or bitterness, or revolt but rather try to help bring about change in whatever small measures that you can (Sandler, 1992, p. 12).

As Rose (1992) stated, "Once you get tenure, enjoy the freedom of academic life," (p. 4). However, if you do not get tenure, recognize that there is life, a lot of life, yet to be lived. Schoenfeld & Magnan (1994) have provided guidelines about what to do if you do not get tenure. Although they believe that no faculty member should theoretically ever run a full six-year obstacle course and then involuntary fail to make tenure (p. 463). They suggested that, in such cases, faculty members who are denied tenure need to closely examine their options. Further, Schoenfeld & Magnan (1994, p. 464-479) believe that there are realistically only four viable options:

1. Try, try again (i.e., take another shot at being successful if, for example, the clock just ran out; there is no tenure-or out ultimatum; the vote was close; etc.);

2. Check out legal avenues (i.e., file an appeal) if you believe that tenure was denied because of some technicality, misunderstanding, or discrimination;

3. Pull out the most recent job list and a good map (i.e., search for greener pastures elsewhere); and,

4. Attempt to build a career in another profession.

Increases in the number of Black women faculty on college and university campuses make us ever mindful of the need for them to find calm, or at least calmer, waters during the tenure process. The experiences of a female assistant professor who reported that the tenure process left her feeling like a gerbil (Verrier, 1993, p. 98), or those of Bell & Nkomo (1999, p. 80), who noted that we should never delude ourselves about our status; we were outsiders even though we had been allowed inside the academy by virtue of our degrees, are testimony to the rough and turbulent waters of the tenure process. Finding calm or calmer waters to be successful in negotiating tenure is essential to the growth in numbers of Black women in the professorate.

References

Allen, R.J. "Advice on managing your successful career." *Nations Restaurant News*, 15 September 1997, 3(37), 30-49.

Arrien, A. *The four-fold way: Walking paths of the warrior, teacher, healer and visionary.* Harper Collins Publishers, Inc., 1993.

Bell, E.E. & Nkomo, S.M. "Postcards from the borderlands: Building a career from the outside/within." *Journal of Career Development* 26 (1): 69-84 (1999).

Bennis, W. "Effective leadership: The exception, not the rule." *U.S. News and World Report*, 25 April 1983.

Bishop, E.G. *Managing in black and white: A guide for the professional woman if color.* Available: http://www.bennett.edu/bw/bwchp4.htm.

Carter, D., Pearson, C. and Shavlik, D. "Double jeopardy: Women of color in higher education." *Educational Record*, Fall 68, 69, 98-103 (1987/88).

Fury, K. "Mentor mania." *Savvy*, 9, 43-49 (1979).

Graves, S.B. "A case of double jeopardy? Black women in higher education." *Initiatives*, 53 (1), 3-8 (1990).

Johnson, G.G. "African American women administrators as mentors: Significance and strategies." *Initiatives*, 58(3), 49-56 (1998).

Kanter, R.M. *Men and women of the corporation.* New York: Basic Books, 1977.

Konrad, A. "New faculty Roles," *Black Issues in Higher Education*, 26 March 1992, 11-13.

Leatherman, C. "Black women in academe," *The Chronicle of Higher Education*, 20 January 1994, A17, 19.

Lindsay, B. "African American women and brown: Twilight or emerging dawn." *Journal of Negro Education*, 63(3), 430-442 1994.

Lowman, J. *Mastering the techniques of teaching.* San Francisco: Jossey-Bass Publishers, 1984.

Moses, Yolanda T. *Black women in academe: Issues and strategies.* Washington, D.C.: Association of American Colleges and Universities. 1989.

Pregent, R. *Charting your course: How to prepare to teach effectively.* Madison, WI: Magna Publications, Inc., 1994.

Rodriguez, M. "Mapping a course for success: University of Arizona's commitment to diversity extends to its non-teaching staff." *Black Issues in Higher Education*, 21 March 1996, 23.

Rose, S. "10 tips to tenure." *Women in Higher Education*, (February 1992): 4.

Sandler, B.R. *Success and Survival Strategies for Women Faculty Members.* Washington, D.C.: Association of American Colleges, 1992.

Schoenfeld A.C. and R. Magnan.. *Mentor in a Manual: Climbing the*

Academic Ladder to Tenure. Madison, WI: Magna Publications, Inc., 1994.

Sellner, E.C. *Mentoring: The Ministry of Spiritual Kinship.* Notre Dame, IN: Ave Maria Press, 1990.

Singh, K, A. Robinson, and J. Williams-Green. "Differences in perceptions of African American women and men faculty and administrator." *Journal of Negro Education,* 64 (4) 401-408.

Smith, E. "Upward mobility: Black and white women administrators." *Journal of NAWDAC,* Spring, 1985.

Southern, V. "The spiritual journey of African American women in higher education." *Thresholds in Education,* 22 (1), 25-32 (1996).

Verrier, D.A. "Perceptions of life on the tenure track." *The NEA Higher Education Journal,* December 1993, 95-124.

Weimer, M., Parrett, J.L. & Kerns, M.M. *How Am I Teaching? Forms and activities for acquiring instructional input.* Madison, WI: Magana Publications, Inc., 1988.

Williams, A. "Research on black women college administrators: Descriptive and interview data." *Sex Roles: A Journal of Research,* 21(1-2), 99-112 (1989).

Wiley, E. "Ability to manage students and collegial expectations key to faculty success," *Black Issues in Higher Education,* 17 December 1992, 3-6.

Zunker, V. *Career Counseling: Applied Concepts of Life Planning.* Pacific Groves, CA: Brooks/Cole Publishing Company, 1998.

Chapter 5

Putting Our Words to Practice

Using Competitive Strategic Planning to Guide You on the Higher Education Ladder of Success

Conchita Y. Battle

Abstract

This essay proposes a model for the integration of competitive strategy and career planning for the purpose of aiding one in achieving a successful career in the field of higher education. This essay will provide a vehicle to use in ones quest. To gain a thorough understanding of the strategy used in the proposed model of competitive strategic analysis it is vital to complete an extensive self-analysis. In attempting to do this it is important to understand what strategic planning and competitive strategy are as they will be applied to higher education career goals.

Introduction

Climbing the ladder of success in higher education is a challenge for women; and it is therefore necessary, for women to approach their career with a strategy using competitive analysis of their goals and outlining all of the possible career options that appear in front of them. This essay proposes a model for the integration of competitive strategy and career planning for the purpose of aiding women in achieving a successful career in the field of higher education. In order to gain a thorough understanding of the strategy used in this model, it is important to understand what strategic planning and competitive strategy are as they will be applied to higher education career goals.

Strategic planning means that one should react actively and not passively to decisions. One needs to look ahead and stay abreast of internal and external environmental changes. According to George Keller (1983), strategic planning is participatory and highly tolerant of controversy. Therefore, this type of planning process will inevitably mean many different things to different people. For some the process is to simply focus on attaining tenure; some may focus on achieving a high level of success in the area of administration or in the area of student development or services. This model proposes comprehensive career planning that takes into account strategic planning and comprehensive analysis of the competitive environment in which one works or intends to work.

Competitive strategy means that one develops a long-range plan which builds on their strengths and helps them to compete more effectively in academe. In order for one to excel in higher education, they must analyze the competition, the type of institution they are interested in working for, and create a unique niche for themselves. Competitive strategy is an on-going process, because the external environment is continuously changing. Change creates new competitive conditions with which one has to contend. Changing external conditions may include new institutional policy regarding tenure, leadership changes, or new programs that other institutions decide to implement. Strategic competitive planning is a positive process, and provides objective measurements for setting personal career goals.

Dealing with the Realities of Planning Your Career: The Process of Self-Analysis

What is your impetus for developing a competitive strategy? What are your goals for a career in higher education? Where are you in your career development as it relates to your goals in higher education?

In answering these questions, you must take into consideration the following aspects and incorporate them into your overall plan of action. Before you begin your self analysis, you must make sure you have a clear perspective of where you are, where you want to be, your limitations of achieving your desired goals, and the strengths you bring to the table. **You must have a vision for yourself.** In addition, you must be ready to: (1) enhance your understanding of your values, strengths and preferences as they relate to your goals in higher education, (2) assess your current level of leadership and development competence, and (3) gain the knowledge, insights and motivation you will need to develop and implement the strategic competitive plan that will serve to enhance your areas of strength, minimize critical weak areas, and improve the fit between you and your desired position.

What is the reality of successfully attaining your intended goals?

You must evaluate where you are now in conjunction with where you want to go. You also have to discover what the essentials will be in order to attain this goal – personally, academically, and physically. What is your timeline? How accessible are you [i.e. family and current work load]? Are you willing to relocate?

Getting Started: Self-Analysis and Discovery

Development of your Competitive Strategic Career Plan

Your plan does not have to be a written document more so than a vision…it should reflect you and the path you set for yourself.   In developing this vision, I have set forth several questions constructed to lead you to begin thinking competitively about your movements towards you desired goals.

Questions to ask yourself:

1.   What are your career goals?

2.   What are the major steps needed to accomplish these goals?

3.   What do you aspire to be ten years from now?

4. What are your strengths?

5. What type of institution are you interested in pursuing? Two-year, four-year, state, private, or a minority serving institution.

6. What geographical locations will you target?

7. How are you different from other academicians in your field of expertise?

8. What new ideas or directions are you heading in or can offer academe?

9. What special role will you play in the higher education network?

10. How are you perceived in the higher education network?

11. What new directions will your area of expertise face within the next five years?

12. Does your competitive strategic career plan build on your strengths? Explain how.

13. Does your plan focus on a particular segment of the student population? What are the characteristics of students you intend to serve? Does your plan take this into account when deciding on the type of institution you which to pursue?

14. In what ways does your competitive strategic career plan recognize other talented people in your field?

15. What are your values and preferences when it comes to your career in academe?

16. What academic areas and college services will be needed in the next decade? Does your strategic plan take this into account? Will it be modified to take this into account?

After answering these questions and creating a unique vision for your particular path, your competitive strategic plan will begin to blossom. Now...let's begin the real journey!

Putting Your Plan To Work

How do you build on the competitive strategic analysis that you have developed for your career goals?

After completing the self-analysis and developing a tentative plan you: (1) should have an enhanced level of introspection, (2) should be aware of how you are perceived by others in the field, (3) should be aware of the impact your values and preferences have in the workplace, (4) should begin to discover and become aware of the motivations behind others' behavior, (5) be able to find a good fit between your strengths, preferences and values at work, and (6) be able to measure change, and use it towards your advantage. If you are unable to assess these six items, it is suggestions that you revisit your self-analysis and seek additional answers for yourself prior to taking the next step. Otherwise, you are ready to begin to look outward and assess how your plan will best fit with the current and future opportunities that lay before you.

Remember, one needs:

- Individual initiative, drive and a vision of success.

- The ability to contend with external influences such as family, changes in leadership, new trends in the field.

- To understand institutional leadership (lack of and/or new appointments).

- Know your institutional constraints (depending on the type of institution).

- External environmental change is occurring daily.

- Ability to move where the moving is the easiest.

- New programs at competitor institutions.

Now that you have tied your self-analysis to external factors and influences and have looked outside of the box. You must project any possible set backs or limitations to your plan.

What are the limitations of your competitive strategic plan? How is this reflected?

Like everything else, things change. Keep abreast to change and adjust your plan accordingly. The major limitations that may surface during your journey may include: (1) effective leadership; (2) institutional vision; (3) adequate information system; (4) effective faculty governance system; (5) incompatible work-family environment; (6) political nuances, and (5) financial stability. When investigating the type of institution in which you which to move towards, look at all of these areas of concern. Rank them in order of importance to you and proceed with the implementation of your plan.

Recommendations

Lessons to be learned from seasoned academicians in the field

Use the voices of those who have experience to aid you in developing your competitive strategic career plan. Common themes and suggestions run throughout *Building Bridges* and have been outlined below. Underneath each lesson is a reference point to where it is discussed in *Building Bridges*. These are lessons we can all walk away with and use daily in our career development. They are as follows:

LESSON #1
Develop a competitive strategic plan early in your career– know the direction in which you are heading and the type of institution in which you may want to work. It is difficult to move between two-year and four-year institutions, as well as between different areas of the country. [SEE APPENDIX 2 and CHARTS 6.1, 6.2, 6.3]

-Gregory; Green/McCloud

LESSON #2
If you are interested in moving towards the presidency, consider attaining a doctorate in an academic discipline instead of attaining a degree in higher education administration. Although there is no set path to the presidency, as seen in Appendix 2, there are several similarities in the route. [SEE APPENDIX 3] Appendix 3 provides a listing of current and former college and university presidents, as well as 35 profiles delineating the paths taken to the presidency. [SEE CHART 6.4]

-Dede/Anderson

LESSON #3
If you are interested in working as an administrator in higher education it is important to attain faculty rank and teach. TEACH. TEACH. TEACH.

LESSON #4
Find a mentor.

-Alejano-Steele; Dede/Anderson; Owens

LESSON #5
Work on developing a good academic reputation in your field. Publish. Research. Actively participate in conferences and forums, etc.

-Gregory; Stokes

LESSON #6
Network. Join associations and relevant organizations. Go to conferences. Get out there. Meet and greet! [SEE APPENDIX I]

-Alejano-Steele; Green/McCloud; Gregory; Owens

LESSON #7
Attain excellent time management skills. Learn how to juggle many tasks at one time. Make it your second nature.

- Green/McCloud

LESSON #8
Understand the culture of the institution in which you choose to work. Know the politics and the history of the institution. Learn who the key players are. Keep your ears and eyes open at all times.

-Price

LESSON #9
Know true strengths and weaknesses of the institution and develop ideas to move it forward. Know your institution and stay ahead of the game. Always have a clear vision of how to lead the pack. Think out of the box.

-Price

LESSON #10
Get used to proving yourself. You are a woman. You are a woman of color. Period.

-Price

LESSON #11
Be aggressive in your competitive strategic planning. No holds barred.

LESSON #12
Establish and maintain good working relationships with your department and other campus constituencies. Let your campus feel your presence.

LESSON #13
Learn how to say 'no'. You can't be everything to everybody. Don't wear yourself thin. Pick and choose and do it well. Go with what will move you forward and closer to your planned goals. Keep your vision in mind.

-Price

LESSON #14
Stay focused in order to accomplish your goals. Don't move from side to side. Always move forward keeping your competitive strategic plan in mind.

LESSON #15
Learn who your friends are.

-Price

LESSON #16
Keep your private, personal business to yourself and off campus.

-Gregory

LESSON #17
Promote your self by becoming your own public relations person.

-Green/McCloud

LESSON #18
Welcome constructive criticism and use it to your advantage.

-Green/McCloud

LESSON #19
Always be prepared.

-Stokes

LESSON #20
Document everything.

-Stokes

LESSON #21
Know the complexities of change and how it relates to group processes.

-Price

LESSON #22
Discipline yourself.

-Gregory

LESSON #23
Find supportive organizational cultures- especially if you are juggling work and family [i.e. non-traditional work-family solutions].

-Wooten/Finley-Hervey

LESSON #24
Learn what your 'spiritual movement of leadership' is.

-Reed

LESSON #25
Determine the scope of your responsibility.

-Fernandez

LESSON #26
Never give up.

-Stokes

LESSON #27
And last but not least, as *Green and McCloud* put it, "Keep your soul
alive."

What are the realities of successfully implementing and accomplishing your competitive strategic plan?

Self analysis and awareness in developing goals is an excellent beginning. But you have to take into account the day-to-day activities of institutional changes and life changes. The institutions in which we choose to work are complex organizations that have to contend with very real situations that can not be put on hold in order to implement a competitive strategic plan. Our daily activities still have to be managed effectively simultaneous with our career planning. Hopefully this essay has brought several points to light that shape the reality of implementing competitive strategic planning as it relates to career paths for woman of color in higher education institutions.

In addition to the lessons learned, one can also take these points away with them when thinking about implementing a competitive strategic planning process.

The literature is good, but the actual practitioners have to do all of the real work. With this in mind, looking at Keller, he outlines important decision-making necessities for institutional leaders to follow and then provides a useful tool for institutional self-analysis. A practitioner will know what strategic planning should be and what the ideal conditions would be for successfully implementing strategic planning, but he does not emphasize all of the additional work and strain this will add to the institution's daily tasks. Keller does mention the need for an institution to hire an external consultant. This will aid a lot of the initial ground work and analysis that needs to be done.

Remember, institutions have a deeper imbedded history and image that is difficult to change. Things are not as cut and dry, it is more difficult for women of color to move past the glass ceiling.

References

Keller, George. *Academic Strategy: The Management Revolution in American Higher Education*. Baltimore: John Hopkins University Press, 1983.

Porter, Michael E. *Competitive Strategy: Techniques for Analyzing Industries and Competitors*. Free Press, 1998.

Conclusion

Coming Together to Build This Bridge

Conchita Y. Battle

As previously discussed, the concept for *Building B ridges* evolved from informal conversations with female, minority colleagues. As a result, Chontrese and I decided it was time to provide a medium for these important voices to be heard. We wanted to create a book that we could have used 10 years ago...before we decided to wade in the water. In addition, we wanted something that would serve as a reference guide we could consult along the various steps. Initially, I did not realize all of the work it would take to get something like this together. I do not think my co-editor did either when she accepted to take on this project. The main challenge for us was locating a diverse group o f women o f c olor i n higher e ducation t hat a ctually h ad t he time to contribute. We had to rely on word of mouth for the majority of our search. We discovered the list of women of color presidents was small...and most of them were African American. We also found, there are still too many first women of color presidents, first women of color tenured faculty, department chairs, etc. We were elated to receive telephone call after telephone call from women in the field that were excited to hear this project had moved beyond the concept phase. Gladly enough, the interest for a project such as this appeared to be great and one that was anticipated by women from all realms of higher education and this served as a motivator for us to continue our pursuit.

The Sections - Thinking Out of the Box

While attempting to provide this practical guide for those seeking careers in the academy, it was important for us as editors to gather all of the information one would need on their journey through the higher education maze and house it in one volume. We divided *Building Bridges* into four distinct areas of concern. We were able to identify and offer ideas to aid the reader in gaining insight of what is expected as well as what to expect on the road to the presidency, general higher education administration positions, faculty nuances, and balancing the role of department chair. Each chapter sets forth new ideas and provides us with traditional and nontraditional outlooks on how to succeed.

In the chapter entitled The Road to the Presidency: Women of Color Assuming Leadership Roles in the Academy, we examined the path to leadership in colleges and universities and outlined methodical steps to the office of the President. Anna Waring began the chapter with her study on career paths traveled by college and university presidents. This study was followed by eloquent personal narratives from current Presidents Fernandez, Freeman, Price and Reed. They all had interesting and uniquely different paths to the presidency. They all concluded with recommendations for any reader interested in pursing a position at the top of the helm of a college or university.

The next chapter, Climatizing Faculty and Administrative Roles: Exploring the Nuances of Minority Serving Institutions and Predominately White Institutions (PWIs) challenged us by making us think out of the box. The authors in this chapter addressed the following issues: barriers women of color face in higher education systems; acceptance in PWIs; challenges faculty face at PWIs; work and family conflict; and politics in higher education. Ultimately, I think we discovered that whether we work at minority serving institutions or PWIs, faculty and administrators face similar issues.

Chapter three, The Department Chair Dichotomy: Balancing Faculty and Administration addressed the balancing act felt by department chairs being split between two worlds, faculty and administration. The chapter clearly identified survival techniques needed to manage the duality of faculty and administrative roles. The contributing papers in this chapter addressed the following questions: What is a typical day-in-the life of a department chair? What is the line of progression to this position? What are the challenges? What are the rewards? What role does mentorship play? What advice would you offer others striving to achieve the same goals?

Wading in the Water: Negotiating the Tenure Process, chapter four, attempted to delineate tenured portfolios and discuss strategies to employ while negotiating the tenure process. Authors outlined expectations, requirements, and meaningful thresholds one needs to be aware of on the pursuit of tenure. Contributing papers discussed and addressed the following: what tenure is; what are the steps needed to attain tenure; challenges faced; and recommendations for success.

In summation, chapter five attempted to provide a hands-on-approach to the advice provided by the contributing authors. A method of evaluating and assessing the readers career and providing a vehicle to guide the reader in moving forward in higher education.

The Writers and What They Bring to the Table

These talented and experienced women have been brought to the table to provide the reader with the benefit of their experience. *Building Bridges* has combined research and personal narratives from women of color currently in the field. They share with the reader their real life challenges and insight from a variety of situations they have faced in higher education. These individual stories shape the foundation of this project and move the issues presented to the next realm of thought and conversation. Not only do the contributing authors lay out their concerns, but the authors eloquently provide possible answers, solutions and recommendations. As editors, we would like to thank these women for their time, dedication and patience.

Using Building Bridges as a Guide

In editing this book, we attempted to examine this culture of aspiration in which we have chosen to work. We were committed to retaining diversity. We truly wanted this book to represent women of color from a wide range of diasporas. We reached out to several communities, and *Building Bridges* is the result.

This was our first project like this and we hope it will spark interest for similar ideas to surface in the future. We hope that *Building*

Bridges will not only begin the discussion on challenges faced by women in higher education, but we hope it provides answers and can serve as a guide for those interested in choosing or continuing a career in higher education.

TABLES

TABLE 1: List of Participating Institutions	
Two Year Institutions	**Four Year Institutions**
College of Eastern Utah	Albany State University
Cuyahoga Community College	Buffalo State University
Georgia Perimeter Community College	Norfolk State University
Northern Virginia Community College	Paine College
Parkland Community College	Southeastern University
Roxbury Community College	University of Nebraska at Kearney

TABLE 2.1:

Actual Number of Minority Females

Per Campus and Percentage Responding Per Campus

Institution	Number of Responses	Total Number of Minority Females on Campus	Response Percentage [%]
Bloomsburg	11	28	39
California	18	31	58
Cheyney	18	95	19
Clarion	8	17	47
East Stroudsburg	10	30	30
Edinboro	10	22	45
Indiana	21	43	49
Kutztown	12	29	41
Lock Haven	8	12	66
Mansfield	6	11	55
Millersville	28	65	43
Shippensburg	18	28	64
Slippery Rock	11	25	44
West Chester	29	122	24
TOTALS	**208**	**558**	**44**

TABLE 2.2: Institution Response Distribution		
Institution	**Number of Responses**	**Percentage** *(Rounded to nearest whole number)*
Bloomsburg	11	5
California	18	9
Cheyney	18	9
Clarion	8	4
East Stroudsburg	10	5
Edinboro	10	5
Indiana	21	10
Kutztown	12	6
Lock Haven	8	4
Mansfield	6	3
Millersville	28	13
Shippensburg	18	9
Slippery Rock	11	5
West Chester	29	14

TABLE 2.3: Work-Family Management Strategies		
Work-Family Management Strategy	**% of Respondents Employing Strategy**	**Examples of Strategies**
Embracing a supportive family-friendly culture at University of employment	26%	The university culture supports the boundaries between work & family The department chair understands the demands of integrating work & family Colleagues are supportive of family obligations Flexible work environment
Utilizing University's formal work-family policies and programs	52%	Maternity leave policy University sponsored Child-Care Centers or Day Camps Stoppage of Tenure Clock for birth of a child Sabbaticals Eldercare referrals
Alternative Career Choices or paths	30%	Part-time faculty member Dual-career Commuter Marriages Arrangement of teaching schedule so that childcare is not provided by non-family members
Integrating Cultural Heritage and Social Support	67%	Seeking out other African-Americans as childcare providers Job relocation near extended family Joining African American organizations for social support Creating informal networks of African American friends

CHARTS

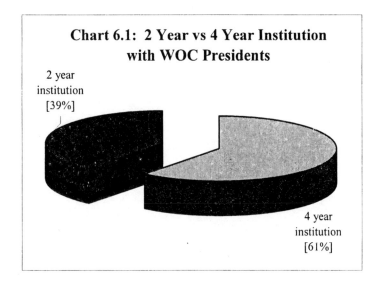

Chart 6.1: 2 Year vs 4 Year Institution with WOC Presidents

2 year institution [39%]

4 year institution [61%]

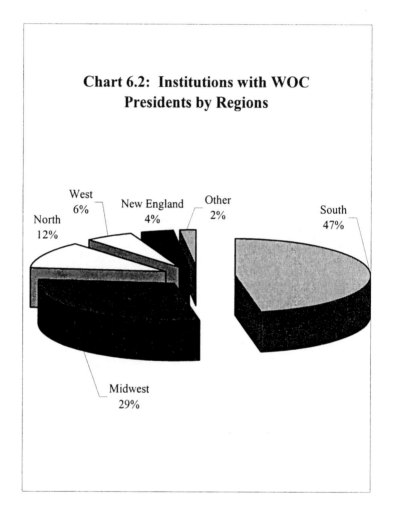

Chart 6.2: Institutions with WOC Presidents by Regions

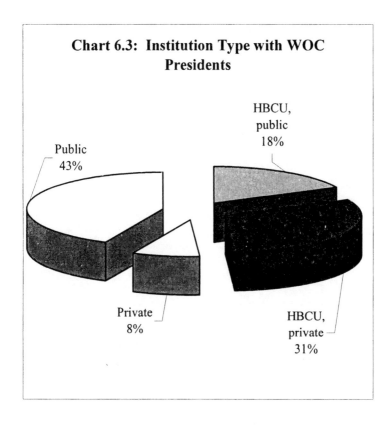

Chart 6.3: Institution Type with WOC Presidents

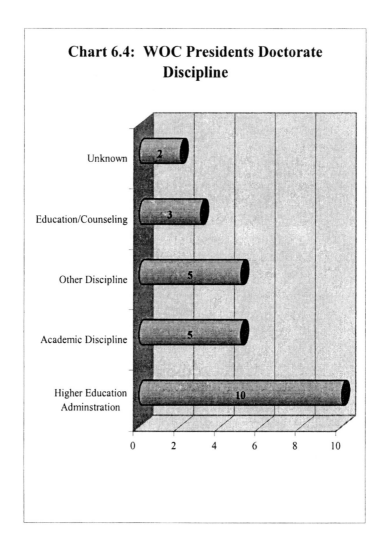

Chart 6.4: WOC Presidents Doctorate Discipline

Unknown 2
Education/Counseling 3
Other Discipline 5
Academic Discipline 5
Higher Education Adminstration 10

0 2 4 6 8 10

APPENDIXES

APPENDIX I

RESOURCES AND CONFERENCE INFORMATION

American Association for Higher Education (AAHE)
One Dupont Circle, N.W., Suite 360, Washington, DC 20036
Telephone: 202.293.6440; Fax: 202.293.0073
Website address: www.aahe.org

American Association of Community Colleges (AACC)
One Dupont Circle, N.W., Suite 410, Washington, DC 20036
Telephone: 202.728.0200; Fax: 202.833.2467

American Association of State Colleges and Universities (AASCU)
One Dupont Circle, N.W., Suite 700, Washington, DC 20036
Telephone: 202.857.1821; Fax: 202.296.5819
Website Address: www.aacc.nche.edu
- *Summer Council of Presidents Meeting*
- *New Presidents Academy*
- *Millennium Leadership Institute*

American Association of University Administrators (AAUP)
P. O. Box 361363, Plano, TX 75026-1363
Telephone: 972.248.3957; Fax: 972.713.8209
Email address: info@allianceedu.org
Website address: www.aaua.org

American Association of University Professors (AAUP)
1012 14th Street, N.W., Suite 500, Washington, DC 20005
Telephone: 202.737.5900, Fax: 202.737.5526
Website Address: www.igc.apc.org/aaup/

American Association of University Women
Forum on Educational Equity
Telephone: 202.728.7609
E-mail address: ERTF@aauw.org

American Council on Education (ACE)

Center for Institutional and International Initiatives
Department Chair Program
One Dupont Circle NW, 8th Floor, Washington, DC 20036-1193
Telephone: 202.939.9343; Fax: 202.785.8056
Website address: www.acenet.edu

Office of Minorities in Higher Education
One Dupont Circle NW, Washington, DC 20036
Telephone: 202.939.9395; Fax: 202.833.5696
E-mail address: omhe@ace.nche.edu

Office of Women in Higher Education
One Dupont Circle NW, Washington, DC 20036
Telephone: 202.939.9390
E-mail address: owhe@ace.nche.edu

Association for the Study of Higher Education

202 Hill Hall, Columbia, MO 65211-2190
Telephone: 573.882.9645, Fax: 573.884.2197
Website address: www.ashe.missouri.edu

Association of American Colleges and Universities (AAC&U)

Office of Diversity, Equity, and Global Initiatives
1818 R Street, N.W., Washington, DC 20009
Telephone: 202.387.3760; Fax: 202.265.9532
Website Address: www.aacu-edu.org

Association of Black Women in Higher Education (ABWHE)

30 Limerick Drive, Albany; NY 12204
Telephone: 518.465.2146

Council of Colleges of Arts and Sciences (CCAS)

▪ Seminar for Department Chairs
▪ Seminar for New Deans
P.O. Box 873108, Tempe, Arizona 85287-3108
Telephone: 480.727.6064, Fax: 480.727.6078
Email address: info@ccas.net
Website address: www.ccas.net

Hispanic Association of Colleges and Universities (HACU)

4204 Gardendale Street, Suite 216, San Antonio, TX 78229
Telephone: 210.692-3805; Fax: 210.692.0823
Website Address: www.incacorp.com/hacu

National Association for Equal Opportunity in Higher Education (NAFEO)
400 12th Street, N.E., Washington, DC 20002
Telephone: 202.543.9111; Fax: 202.543.9113
Website address: www.nafeo.org

National Association for Women in Catholic Higher Education (NAWCHE)
Women's Studies Program, Sociology Department
519A McGuinn Hall, Boston College, Chestnut Hill, MA 02467
Telephone: 617.552.4198; Fax: 617.552.4283
Email address: nawche@bc.edu

National Association of College and University Business Officers (NACUBO)
One Dupont Circle, N.W., Suite 500, Washington, DC 20036
Telephone: 202.861.2514; Fax: 202.861.2583
Website Address: www.nacubo.org

National Association of Student Personnel Administrators (NASPA)
Personal Effectiveness Institute (National Academy for Leadership and Executive Effectiveness)
1875 Connecticut Avenue, N.W., Suite 418, Washington, DC 20009-5728
Telephone: 202-265-7500; Fax: 202.797.1157
Website Address: www.naspa.org

National MultiCultural Institute
3000 Connecticut Avenue NW, Suite 438, Washington, DC 20008-2556
Telephone: 202.483.0700; Fax: 202.483.5233
E-mail address: nmci@nmci.org
Website address: www.nmci.org

Southern Oregon Women in Higher Education Conference
Telephone: 541.552.6668
Website Address: www.sou.edu/sowhe

Southwest Center for Human Relations Studies
Annual National Conference on Race & Ethnicity in American Higher Education (NCORE)
Public and Community Services Division, College of Continuing Education
The University of Oklahoma
2350 McKown Drive
Norman, Oklahoma 73072-6678

Telephone: 405.292.4172; Fax: 405.292.4177
Website address: www.occe.ou.edu/NCORE

Summer Institute for Women in Higher Education Administration
Bryn Mawr College
101 N. Merion Avenue, Bryn Mawr, PA 19010 - 2899
Telephone: 610.526.7325; Fax: 610.526.7327
Website address: www.brynmawr.edu/summerinstitute/

APPENDIX 2

ROAD TO THE PRESIDENCY

Archie-Hudson, Marguerite	Education		
Presidency	Bachelor's	Master's	Doctorate (PhD)
Talladega College	Talladega College	Harvard University	University of California, Los Angeles
	Psychology		*Higher Education Administration*

Professional Road to the Presidency
Director, Education Opportunity Program, California State University
Associate Dean, College of Letters & Sciences, University of California, Los Angeles
Chief of Staff, Speaker Willie Brown
Chief of Staff, Congresswoman Yvonne Brathwaite-Burke Assemblywoman, California State Legislature
Public Policy Consultant
Board Member, Talladega College Board of Trustees
President, Talladega College
Independent Consultant, Archie-Hudson & Associates
Assemblywoman, California State Legislature

Banks, Elvalee	Education		
Presidency	**Bachelor's**	**Master's**	**Doctorate (PhD)**
Mary Holmes College	Ohio State University	Ohio State University	University of Minnesota
	Early Childhood Education	*Student Personnel Administration*	*Educational Administration*
Professional Road to the Presidency			
Adjunct Professor, Bowie State University Director of Institutional Analysis, Coppin State University Chief Planner, Jackson State University Executive Assistant to the President, Jackson State University **President, Mary Holmes College** Academic Affairs, Wilberforce University			

Boyd-Scotland, Joann R.G.	Education		
Presidency	**Bachelor's**	**Master's**	**Doctorate (PhD)**
Denmark Technical College	Tougaloo College	Jackson State University	Kansas State University, Manhattan
	Psychology & Music Education	*Education Guidance & Counseling*	*Education/ Curriculum & Institutional Administration*
Professional Road to the Presidency			

Executive Director, South Carolina Curriculum Congress
Director of Graduate Studies, Lander University
Professor of Education, Lander University
Dean, School of Education, Lander University
President, Denmark Technical College

Cole, Johnnetta B.	Education		
Presidency	**Bachelor's**	**Master's**	**Doctorate (PhD)**
Spelman College	Oberlin College	Northwestern University	Northwestern University
Bennett College		*Anthropology*	*Education/ Curriculum & Institutional Administration*

Professional Road to the Presidency
Assistant Professor, University of California, Los Angeles
Assistant Professor of Anthropology, Washington State University, Pullman
Director of Black Studies Program, Washington State University, Pullman
Professor, Anthropology & African American Studies, University of Massachusetts at Amherst
Associate Provost for Undergraduate Education, University of Massachusetts at Amherst
Professor of Anthropology, Hunter College
Director of the Latin American & Caribbean Studies Program, Hunter College
Professor, City University of New York
President, Spelman College
Presidential Distinguished Professor of Anthropology, Women's Studies, & African American Studies, Emory University
Presidential Appointment, Commission on the Celebration of Women in History
Governor Appointment, Education Reform Study Commission
President, Bennett College

Collins, Althia	Education		
Presidency	Bachelor's	Master's	Doctorate (Ed.D.)
Bennett College		The University of Tennessee	The University of Tennessee
		English Education	*Educational Administration & Supervision*
Professional Road to the Presidency			
Instructor, English			
Assistant Professor, English			
Associate Professor, English			
Executive Assistant to the President, SUNY Health Science Center			
Assistant Vice President for Academic Affairs, Mankato State University			
Vice President Academic Affairs, United States International University			
CEO/Founder, Academic and Educational Resources, Consulting Firm			
President, Bennett College			

Copeland, Elaine Johnson	Education		
Presidency	**Bachelor's**	**Master's**	**Doctorate (PhD)**
Clinton Junior College	Livingstone College	Winthrop University **(MAT)**	Oregon State University
		University of Illinois **(MBA)**	*Counseling*

Professional Road to the Presidency
Professor of Business, Clinton Junior College

Chair, Business Department, Clinton Junior College
Associate Dean of the Graduate College,
　University of Illinois, Urbana-Champaign
Associate Vice Chancellor for Academic Affairs,
　University of Illinois, Urbana-Champaign
Vice President/Dean for Academic Affairs,
　Livingstone College
Associate Professor Emerita, Educational Psychology,
　University of Illinois, Urbana-Champaign
Acting President, Clinton Junior College
President, Clinton Junior College

Daniel, Elnora D.	Education		
Presidency	**Bachelor's**	**Master's (Med)**	**Doctorate (Ed.D.)**
Chicago State University		Teacher's College, Columbia University	Teacher's College, Columbia University

Professional Road to the Presidency

Director, School of Nursing, Hampton University
Dean, School of Nursing, Hampton University
Vice President for Academic Affairs, Hampton University
Vice President for Health
Executive Vice President and Provost
President, Chicago State University

Dorsey, Myrtle E.B.	Education		
Presidency	**Bachelor's**	**Master's (Med)**	**Doctorate (Ed.D.)**
Baton Rouge Community College	Morgan State University	Morgan State University	University of Texas
	Spanish & Education	*Reading Specialist*	*Higher Education Administration*

Professional Road to the Presidency
Towson State University
Bowie State University
University of Maryland, College Park
Howard Community College
Vice President for Student Affairs,
Baltimore City Community College
Vice President for Student Affairs and Institutional
Advancement, Georgia Perimeter College
Executive Vice President,
Cincinnati State Technical and Community College
President, Baton Rouge Community College

Farris, Vera King	Education		
Presidency	**Bachelor's**	**Master's**	**Doctorate (PhD)**
Richard Stockton College of New Jersey	Tuskegee University *Biology*	University of Massachusetts *Zoology Parasitology*	University of Massachusetts *Zoology Parasitology*

Professional Road to the Presidency

Research Scientist & Faculty member, University of Michigan
Dean, State University of New York, Stony Brook
Research Scientist & Faculty member,
   State University of New York, Stony Brook
Vice President for Academic Affairs,
   State University of New York, Brockport
Research Scientist & Faculty member,
   State University of New York, Brockport
Academic Vice President, Kean College
President, Richard Stockton College of New Jersey

Freeman, Algeania Warren	Education		
Presidency	**Bachelor's**	**Master's**	**Doctorate (PhD)**
Livingstone College	Fayetteville State University	Southern Illinois University	The Ohio State University
	English	*Speech Pathology & Audiology*	*Speech Communications*

Professional Road to the Presidency
Instructor, Norfolk State University Morgan State University East Tennessee State University Orange Coast College North Carolina AT&T University **President, Livingstone College**

Hughes, Marvalene	Education		
Presidency	Bachelor's	Master's	Doctorate (PhD)
California State University, Stanislaus	Tuskeegee University	New York University *Columbia University*	Florida State University *Counseling & Administration*

Professional Road to the Presidency

Vice President for Student Affairs/Vice Provost,
  University of Minnesota
Professor of Educational Psychology,
  University of Minnesota
Vice President/Professor, University of Toledo
Associate Vice President, Arizona State University
San Diego State University
President, California State University, Stanislaus

Jarvis, Charlene Drew	Education		
Presidency	**Bachelor's**	**Master's**	**Doctorate (PhD)**
Southeastern University	Oberlin College	Howard University	University of Maryland *Neuropsychology*
Professional Road to the Presidency			
Research Scientist, National Institute of Mental Health Councilwoman, District of Columbia **President, Southeastern University**			

Jones, Grace Sawyer	Education		
Presidency	**Bachelor's**	**Master's**	**Doctorate (PhD)**
College of Eastern Utah	Washburn University	George Williams College	Union Institute
Three Rivers Community College	*Physical Education*	*Community Recreation & Anthropology*	*Organizational Behavior*
Professional Road to the Presidency			

Secondary Teacher, Physical Education, Chicago, IL
Faculty/Coordinator of the Recreational Leadership Program,
  Berkshire Community College
Coordinator of Student Activities & Student Union,
  Berkshire Community College
Director of Personnel Services, Berkshire Community College
Professor (tenured), SUNY, College of Oneonta
Vice President for Multicultural Affairs, SUNY,
  College of Oneonta
President, College of Eastern Utah
President, Three Rivers Community College			

Kennedy, Yvonne	Education		
Presidency	**Associate's/ Bachelor's**	**Master's**	**Doctorate (PhD)**
Bishop State Community College	Bishop State Community College **(AA)**	Morgan State University	The University of Alabama
	English	*English*	*Higher Education Administration*
	Alabama State University **(BA)**		
	English-Social Science/French		

Professional Road to the Presidency
Instructor, Bishop State Community College
Coordinator for Cooperative Programs/Education Improvement Programs, Bishop State Community College
Associate Director for Cooperative Programs/EIP, Bishop State Community College
Coordinator of Title III Programs, Bishop State Community College
President, Bishop State Community College
House of Representatives, State of Alabama

Manley, Audrey Forbes	Education		
Presidency	**Bachelor's**	**Master's**	**Doctorate (MD)**
Spelman College	Spelman College	John Hopkins University *Public Health*	Meharry Medical College

Professional Road to the Presidency

Pediatrician, Chicago
Faculty, Medical pediatrics, Chicago Medical College
Faculty, Medical pediatrics, University of Illinois
Faculty/Hospital administration, Medical pediatrics,
   University of Chicago
Faculty/Hospital administration, Medical Pediatrics,
   University of California, San Francisco
Faculty/Hospital administration, Medical Pediatrics,
   Emory University
Commissioned Officer, Public Health Practice & Public Health
   Services, Department of Health & Human Services,
   John Hopkins University
Faculty, Medical Pediatrics, Howard University
Principal Deputy Assistant Secretary for Health
Assistant United States Surgeon General
Deputy Assistant Secretary of Health
Deputy United States Surgeon General
Acting Surgeon General
President, Spelman College

McDemmond, Marie	Education		
Presidency	**Bachelor's**	**Master's**	**Doctorate (PhD)**
Norfolk State University	Xavier University	University of New Orleans	University of Massachusetts, Amherst

Professional Road to the Presidency

Director, Higher Education Opportunity Program,
  College of New Rochelle
Assistant Professor, Higher Education Finance/Management,
  University of New Orleans
Acting Deputy Director & Business Officer,
  Bronx Psychiatric Center
Associate, New York State Board of Regents
Assistant Vice President for Finance, Emory University
Associate Vice President for Administration & Finance &
  Budget Director, University of Massachusetts, Amherst
Vice President for Budget and Finance, Clark Atlanta University
Vice President for Budget and Finance,
  Florida Atlantic University
President, Norfolk State University

Moses, Yolanda T.	Education		
Presidency	**Associate's/ Bachelor's**	**Master's**	**Doctorate (PhD)**
The City College of New York	San Bernardino Valley College **(AA)**	University of California, Riverside	University of California, Riverside
American Association for Higher Education	California State University, San Bernardino **(BA)**	*Anthropology*	*Anthropology*
	Sociology		

Professional Road to the Presidency

Professor of Anthropology, The City College of New York
Professor of Anthropology, CUNY Graduate School
Dean, California State Polytechnic University, Pomona
Professor of Anthropology,
  California State Polytechnic University, Pomona
Vice President for Academic Affairs,
  California State University, Dominguez Hills
Professor of Anthropology,
  California State University, Dominguez Hills
President, The City College of New York
President, American Association for Higher Education

Pettigrew, L. Eudora	Education		
Presidency	Bachelor's	Master's	Doctorate (PhD)
State University of New York at Old Westbury			

Professional Road to the Presidency

Instructor, Swift Memorial Junior College
Instructor, Southern Illinois University
Associate Professor of Psychology, University of Bridgeport
Professor of Urban Affairs and Public Policy,
   Michigan State University
Associate Provost for Instruction, University of Delaware
President, State University of New York at Old Westbury

Ragster, LaVerne	Education		
Presidency	Bachelor's	Master's	Doctorate (PhD)
University of the Virgin Islands	University of Miami	San Diego State University	University of California, San Diego
	Biology & Chemistry	*Biology*	*Biology*

Professional Road to the Presidency
Assistant Professor, Marine Biology, University of the Virgin Islands
Professor, Marine Biology, University of the Virgin Islands
Chair, Division, Science & Mathematics, University of the Virgin Islands
Acting Vice President for Research & Land Grant Affairs, University of the Virgin Islands
Vice President for Research & Public Service, University of the Virgin Islands
Senior Vice President/Provost, University of the Virgin Islands
President, University of the Virgin Islands

Runnels, Angie Stokes	Education		
Presidency	Bachelor's	Master's	Doctorate (PhD)
St. Philip's College	Butler College	East Texas State University	The University of Texas, Austin
	English	*Education*	*Educational Administration*

Professional Road to the Presidency
Elementary teacher, English/Reading High School teacher, English/Reading Instructor, English Instructional Dean Vice President for Student Affairs, North Lake College Vice President for Academic Affairs, North Lake College Interim President, North Lake College Executive Director of Educational Partnerships, Dallas Community College District **President, St. Philip's College**

Scott, Gloria Randle	Education		
Presidency	**Bachelor's**	**Master's**	**Doctorate (PhD)**
Bennett College	Indiana University	Indiana University	Indiana University
	Zoology	*Zoology*	*Higher Education*

Professional Road to the Presidency

Research Associate, Genetics & Embryology, Indiana University
Instructor, Biology, Marian College
Dean of Students & Director of Upward Bound,
   Knoxville College
Special Assistant to the President,
   North Carolina AT&T University
Director of Educational Research/Planning,
   North Carolina AT&T University
Director of Educational Planning, Evaluation,
   Texas Southern University
Bryn Mawr College
Grambling State University
Executive Vice President, Clark College
President, Bennett College
President and owner, G. Randle Services

Shields, Portia Holmes	Education		
Presidency	**Bachelor's**	**Master's**	**Doctorate (PhD)**
Albany State University	District of Columbia Teachers College	George Washington University	The University of Maryland, College Park
	Education	*Education*	*Early Childhood & Elementary Education*

Professional Road to the Presidency

Elementary teacher, Reading Specialist
High School teacher, Reading Specialist
Instructor for Upward Bound
Director of the College of Medicine, Medical & Biomedical
  Communications, Howard University
Dean of the School of Education, Howard University
President, Albany State University

Simmons, Ruth J.	Education		
Presidency	**Bachelor's**	**Master's**	**Doctorate (PhD)**
Smith College Brown University	Dillard University	Harvard University *Romance Languages/ Literatures*	Harvard University *Romance Languages/ Literatures*

Professional Road to the Presidency

Assistant Professor, French, University of New Orleans
Assistant Dean for the College of Liberal Arts,
   University of New Orleans
Visiting Associate Professor of Pan-African Studies,
   California State University, Northridge
Acting Director of International Programs,
   California State University, Northridge
Assistant Dean of Graduate Studies,
   University of Southern California
Associate Dean for Graduate Studies,
   University of Southern California
Director of Afro-American Studies, Princeton University
Associate Dean of Faculty, Princeton University
Provost, Spelman College
Vice Provost, Princeton University
President, Smith College
President, Brown University

Slade, Priscilla Dean	Education		
Presidency	**Bachelor's**	**Master's**	**Doctorate (PhD)**
Texas Southern University	Mississippi State University	Jackson State University	University of Texas, Austin
	Business Administration	*Professional Accounting*	*Accounting*

Professional Road to the Presidency

Chair, Accounting Department, Texas Southern University
Dean, School of Business, Texas Southern University
Acting President, Texas Southern University
President, Texas Southern University

Suber, Dianne Boardley	Education		
Presidency	Bachelor's	Master's	Doctorate (PhD)
Saint Augustine's College	Hampton University	University of Illinois, Urbana	Virginia Polytechnic Institute & State University
	Early Childhood Education	*Curriculum Development*	*Educational Administration*

Professional Road to the Presidency
Teacher Elementary Principal Secondary Principal Adjunct Professor, Graduate College of Education, Hampton University Dean of Administrative Services, Hampton University Assistant Provost, Hampton University Assistant Provost, Hampton University Vice President for Administrative Services, Hampton University **President, Saint Augustine's College**

Surles, Carol Diann	Education		
Presidency	**Bachelor's**	**Master's**	**Doctorate (Ed.D.)**
Texas Woman's University Eastern Illinois University	Fisk University *Psychology*	Chapman University *Counseling*	University of Michigan

Professional Road to the Presidency

University of Central Florida
Vice Chancellor for Administration, University of Michigan
Vice President for Academic Affairs, Jackson State University
Professor of Management, Jackson State University
Vice President for Administration & Business Affairs,
    California State University, Haywood
Visiting Executive in Residence,
    California State University, Haywood
President, Texas Woman's University
President, Eastern Illinois University

Sudarkasa, Niara	Education		
Presidency	**Bachelor's**	**Master's**	**Doctorate (PhD)**
Lincoln University	Oberlin College	Columbia University *Anthropology*	Columbia University *Anthropology*

Professional Road to the Presidency

Columbia University
Assistant Professor, New York University
Assistant Professor, University of Michigan, Ann Arbor
Associate Professor, University of Michigan, Ann Arbor
Professor, University of Michigan, Ann Arbor
Director of the Center for Afro-American Studies,
   University of Michigan, Ann Arbor
Research Scientist, Center for Research on Economic Development, University of Michigan, Ann Arbor
Associate Vice President for Academic Affairs,
   University of Michigan, Ann Arbor
President, Lincoln University
Distinguished Visiting Scholar, Florida Atlantic University

Tatum, Beverly Daniel	Education		
Presidency	**Bachelor's**	**Master's**	**Doctorate (PhD)**
Mount Holyoke College (Acting) Spelman College	Wesleyan University *Psychology*	University of Michigan *Clinical Psychology*	University of Michigan *Clinical Psychology*
Professional Road to the Presidency			
Lecturer, Department of Black Studies, University of California, Santa Barbara Assistant Professor, Westfield State College Associate Professor, Westfield State College Dean, Mount Holyoke College Acting President, Mount Holyoke College **President, Spelman College**			

Thornton, Jerry Sue	Education		
Presidency	**Bachelor's**	**Master's**	**Doctorate (PhD)**
Lakewood Community College	Murray State University	Murray State University	University of Texas at Austin
Cuyahoga Community College			

Professional Road to the Presidency
Junior High School teacher, Earlington, Kentucky
High School Teacher, Kentucky
Dean of Arts and Sciences, Triton College at River Grove
President, Lakewood Community College
President, Cuyahoga Community College

Warner, Neari F.	Education		
Presidency	**Bachelor's**	**Master's**	**Doctorate (PhD)**
Grambling State University (Acting)	Grambling State University	Clark Atlanta University *English Education*	Louisiana State University *Curriculum & Instruction*

Professional Road to the Presidency
Coordinator of TRIO Programs, Southern University
Associate Professor, Southern University
Director of Upward Bound, Southern University
Dean of the Junior Division, Southern University
Acting Vice President for Academic Affairs, Grambling State University
Special Assistant to the President, Grambling State University
Vice President for Development & University Relations, Grambling State University
Interim Vice President for Student Affairs, Grambling State University
Assistant Vice President for Academic Affairs, Grambling State University
Acting President, Grambling State University

Wheelan, Belle S.	Education		
Presidency	**Bachelor's**	**Master's**	**Doctorate (PhD)**
Central Virginia Community College	Trinity University	Louisiana State University	University of Texas
Northern Virginia Community College	*Psychology & Sociology*	*Developmental Educational Psychology*	*Educational Administration*
Professional Road to the Presidency			
Director of Developmental Education, San Antonio College Director of Academic Support Services, San Antonio College Dean of Student Services, Thomas Nelson Community College Provost, Tidewater Community College **President, Central Virginia Community College** **President, Northern Virginia Community College** Secretary of Education, Commonwealth of Virginia			

Wilson, Blenda J.	Education		
Presidency	**Bachelor's**	**Master's**	**Doctorate (PhD)**
California State University, Northridge Nellie Mae Education Foundation	Cedar Crest College *English & Secondary Education*	Seton Hall University *Education*	Boston College *Higher Education* *Administration*

Professional Road to the Presidency
Rutgers University Senior Associate Dean, Graduate School of Education, Harvard University Vice President, Effective Sector, Independent Sector Executive Director, Colorado Commission on Higher Education Chancellor, University of Michigan, Dearborn **President, California State University, Northridge** President/CEO, Nellie Mae Education Foundation

Yancy, Dorothy Cowser	Education		
Presidency	**Bachelor's**	**Master's**	**Doctorate**
Johnson C. Smith University	Johnson B. Smith University	University of Massachusetts, Amherst	Atlanta University
	History & Social Science	*History*	*Political Science*

Professional Road to the Presidency
Teacher, Evanston Township High School
Instructor, Barat College
Faculty, Hampton University
Faculty, Albany State University
Associate Director, School of Social Science, Georgia Institute of Technology
Associate Professor, History, Technology and Society, School of Management, Georgia Institute of Technology
Professor, History, Technology and Society, School of Management, Georgia Institute of Technology
President, Johnson C. Smith University

APPENDIX 3

WOMAN OF COLOR PRESIDENTS [PAST AND PRESENT]

Marguerite Archie-Hudson
Former- Talladega College
Independent Consultant, Archie-Hudson and Associates
Charleston, SC

Elvalee Banks
Former - Mary Holmes College

Joann R. G. Boyd-Scotland
Denmark Technical College
Soloman Blatt, P.O. Box 327, Denmark, SC 29042
Website address: www.den.tec.sc.us

Irma Hunter Brown
Former -Shorter College
Politician- Arkansas Senator

Cecilia Cervantes
College of Alameda
555 Atlantic Avenue, Alameda, CA 94501
Telephone: 510.522.7221 x2200; Fax: 510.522.6019
Email: ccervantes@peralta.cc.ca.us
Website: www.peralta.cc.ca.us

Johnnetta B. Cole
Former – Spelman College
Bennett College
900 East Washington Street, Greensboro, NC 27401
Telephone: 336.517.2225; Fax: 336.370.8633
Email : jbc@sprintmail.com
Website address: www.bennett.edu

Althia Collins
Former - Bennett College

Elaine Johnson Copeland
Clinton Junior College
1029 Crawford Road, Rock Hill, SC 29732

Telephone: 803.327.7402; Fax: 803.327.3261
Email address: ecopeland@clintonjrcollege.org
Website address: www.clintonjrcollege.org

Delores E. Cross
Former-Morris Brown College

Elnora D. Daniel
Chicago State University
10400 South Longwood Drive, Chicago, IL 60643
Telephone: 773.779.0731; Fax: 773.995.3849
Website address: www.csu.edu

Myrtle E. B. Dorsey
Baton Rouge Community College
5310 Florida Boulevard, Baton Rouge, LA 70806
Telephone: 225.216.8402
Website address: www.brcc.cc.la.us

Vera King Farris
Richard Stockton College of New Jersey
P.O. Box 195, Pomona, NJ 08240
Telephone: 609.652.1776
Website address: www.stockton.edu/stockton

Dolores M. Fernández
Eugenio María de Hostos Community College
of The City University of New York
500 Grand Concourse, Bronx, NY 10451
Telephone: 718.518.4444
Email address: dfernandez@hostos.cuny.edu
Website address: www.hostos.cuny.edu

Algeania Warren Freeman
Livingstone College and Hood Theological Seminary
701 West Monroe Street, Salisbury, NC 28144
Telephone: 704.216.6152; Fax: 704.216.6217
Website address: www.livingstone.edu

Marjorie Harris
Lewis College of Business
17370 Meyers Road, Detroit, MI 48235
Telephone: 313.862.6300 x222; Fax: 313. 862.1027
Website address: www.lewiscollege.edu

Zelma Harris
Parkland College
2400 West Bradley Avenue, Champaign, Illinois 61821
Telephone: 217.351.2200
Website address: www.parkland.cc.il.us

Barbara Hatton
Knoxville College
901 College Street, Knoxville, TN 37921
Telephone: 865.524.6511/6836; Fax: 865.524.6603
Website address: www.knoxvillecollege.edu

Beverly W. Hogan
Tougaloo College
500 West County Line Road, Tougaloo, MS 39174
Telephone: 601.977.7730; Fax: 601.977.7739
Email address: Beverly.Hogan@tougaloo.edu
Website address: www.tougaloo.edu

Marvalene Hughes
California State University, Stanislaus
801 West Monte Vista Avenue, Turlock, CA 95382
Telephone: 209. 667.3201
E-mail: Hughes_Marvalene@macmail.csustan.edu
Website address: www.csustan.edu

Charlene Drew Jarvis
Southeastern University
501 I Street, SW, Washington, DC 20024
Telephone: 202.488.8162; Fax: 202.488.8093
Email: president@admin.seu.edu
Website address: www.seu.edu

Sebetha Jenkins
Jarvis Christian College
U.S. Highway 80, P.O. Box 1470, Hawkins, TX 75765-1470
Telephone: 903.769.5882; Fax: 903.769.4842
Website address: www.jarvis.edu

Grace Sawyer Jones
Former – College of Eastern Utah
Three Rivers Community College
7 Mahan Drive, Norwich, CT 06360
Telephone: 860.886.0177

Website address: www.trcc.commnet.edu

Yvonne Kennedy
Bishop State Community College
Mobile, AL 36603
Telephone: 251.690.6416; Fax: 251.438.9523
Email Address: ykennedy@bscc.cc.al.us
Website address: www.bscc.cc.al.us

Elva Concha LeBlanc
Galveston College
4015 Avenue Q, Galveston, TX 77550-7496
Telephone: 409.763.6551, ext. 200; Fax: 409.762.9367
Website: www.gc.edu

Shirley A. R. Lewis
Paine College
1235 Fifteenth Street, Augusta, Georgia 30901-3182
Telephone: 706.821.8230; Fax: 706.821.8333
Email address: lewiss@mail.paine.edu
Website address: www.paine.edu

Adena Williams Loston
San Jacinto College South
13735 Beamer Road, Houston, TX 77089-6099
Telephone: 281.922.3400
Website address: www.sjcd.cc.tx.us

Audrey Forbes Manley
Former- Spelman College

Helen T. McAlpine
J.F. Drake State Technical College
3421 Meridian Street, N, Huntsville, AL 35811
Telephone: 256.539.8161 x100; Fax: 256.539.7383
Website address: www.dstc.cc.al.us

Marie V. McDemmond
Norfolk State University
700 Park Avenue, Norfolk, VA 23504 USA
Telephone: 757.823.8670; Fax: 757.823.2342
Email address: president@nsu.edu
Website address: www.nsu.edu

Yolanda T. Moses
Former – The City College of New York
President, American Association of Higher Education

L. Eudora Pettigrew
Former- State University of New York at Old Westbury

Shirley R. Pippins
Thomas Nelson Community College
P.O. Box 9407, Hampton, Virginia 23670
Telephone: 757.518.4294
Email address: pippinss@tncc.vccs.edu
Website address: www.tncc.cc.va.us

Vivian M. Presley
Coahoma Community College
3240 Friars Point Road, Clarksdale, MS 38614
Telephone: 662.621.4130; Fax: 662.624.9516
Email address: ccci@gmi.net
Website address: www.ccc.cc.ms.us

Glenda D. Price
Marygrove College
8425 West McNichols Road, Detroit, MI 48221-2599
Telephone: 313.927.1200
Email: gprice@marygrove.edu
Website address: www.marygrove.edu

Laverne E. Ragster
University of the Virgin Islands
Charlotte Malie, St. Thomas, US VI 00802
Telephone: 340.693.1000; Fax: 340.693.1005
Website address: www.uvi.edu

Trudie Kibbe Reed
Philander Smith College
812 West 13th Street, Little Rock, AR 72202
Email address: treed@philander.edu
Website address: www.philander.edu

Carolyn Reid-Wallace
Fisk University
1000 17th Avenue, North, Nashville, TN 37208
Telephone: 615.329.8555; Fax: 615.329.8576
Email address: jlsmith@dubois.fisk.edu

Website address: www.fisk.edu

Angie Stokes Runnels
Saint Philip's College
1801 Martin Luther King, Jr. Drive, San Antonio, TX 78203
Telehone: 210.531.359; Fax : 210.531.3590
Website address: www.accd.edu/spc/spcmain/spc

Cynthia McCullough Russell
Former - Clinton Junior College

Gloria Adean Randle Scott
Former- Bennett College
Consultant, G. Randle Services

Mária C. Sheehan
College of the Desert
43-500 Monterey Avenue, Palm Desert, CA 92260
Telephone: 760.773.2500; Fax: 760.341.9732
Email: msheehan@dccd.cc.ca.us
Websitewww.collegeofthedesert.edu

Portia Holmes Shields
Albany State University
504 College Drive, Albany, Ga. 31705
Telephone: 292.430.2799; Fax: 292.430.3836
Website: asuweb.asurams.edu/asu

Ruth J. Simmons
Former – Smith College
Brown University
Box 1860, Providence, Rhode Island 02910
Telephone: 401.863.2234; Fax: 401.863.7737
Website address: www.brown.edu

Pricilla Dean Slade
Texas Southern University
3100 Cleburne Avenue, Houston, Texas 77004
Telephone: 713.313.7035; Fax: 713.313.1092
Website address: www.tsu.edu

Dolores R. Spikes
Former - University of Maryland Eastern Shore

Gwendolyn W. Stephenson
Hillsborough Community College
Email: gstephenson@hcc.cc.fl.us
Website address: www.hcc.cc.fl.us

Dianne Boardley Suber
Saint Augustine's College
1315 Oakwood Avenue, Raleigh, NC 27610-2298
Telephone: 919.516.4200; Fax: 919.828.0817
Email address: dsuber@es.st-aug.edu
Website address: www.st-aug.edu

Niara Sudarkasa
Former -Lincoln University
Distinguished Visiting Scholar, Florida Atlantic University

Carol Diann Surles
Former – Texas Women's University
Former -Eastern Illinois University

Beverly Daniel Tatum
Spelman College
350 Spelman Lane SW, Atlanta, GA 30314
Telephone: 404.223.1400; Fax: 404.223.7523
Email: btatum@spelman.edu
Web site: www.spelman.edu

Thelma Thompson
University of Maryland, Eastern Shore
Princess Anne, MD 21853
Telephone: 410.651.6349
Email: tbthompson@mail.umes.edu
Website address: www.umes.edu

Jerry Sue Thornton
Cuyahoga Community College
700 Carnegie Avenue, Cleveland, OH 44115
Telephone: 216.987.4850
Email: jerry-sue.thornton@tri-c.cc.oh.us
Website: www.tri-c.cc.oh.us

Neari F. Warner
Grambling State University
Main Street, Grambling, LA 71245
Telephone: 318.274.6117, Fax: 318.274.6172

Email address: nfwarner@martin.gram.edu
Website address: www.gram.edu

Belle S. Wheelan
Former - Northern Virginia Community College
Virginia Secretary of Education

Carolyn Williams
Bronx Community College
City University of New York
Bronx, NY 10453
Email address: Carolyn.Williams@bcc.cuny.edu
Website address: www.bcc.cuny.edu

Blenda J. Wilson
Former- California State University, Northridge
President, Nellie Mae Education Foundation
1250 Hancock Street, Suite 205N, Quincy, MA 02169
Telephone: 781.348.4200; Fax: 781.348.4299
Email address: bwilson@nmefdn.org
Website address: www.nelliemaefoundation.org/

Dorothy Cowser Yancy
Johnson C. Smith University
100 Beatties Ford Road, Charlotte, NC 28216
Telephone: 704.378.1007; Fax: 704.372.5746
Email address: dcyancy@jcsu.edu
Website address: www.jcsu.edu

INDEX

American Association of State Colleges and Universities (AASCU), 193
American Association of University Administrators (AAUP), 193
American Association of University Professors (AAUP), 106, 193
  1940 Statement of Principles, 149
  tenure statistics and, 149
American Association of University Women, 193
American Council on Education (ACE), 106, 194
Anderson, Carol
  and acceptance of minorities in the campus community, 59
  and *Perceptions of Minority Women Employed By a State System of Higher Education*, 51-60
  and *The Case of Female Diversity in a University State System*, 49
Archie-Hudson, Marguerite, 230
  professional background of, 197
Asian Pacific American in Higher Education Conference, 106
Association for the Study of Higher Education, 194
Association of American Colleges and Universities, 194
Association of Black Women in Higher Education (ABWHE), 194

B

Banks, Elvalee, 230
  professional background of, 199
Battle, Conchita Y.
  and *Coming Together to Build This Bridge*, 181-184
  and Thinking Out of the Box, 181-183
  and *Using Competitive Strategic Planning to Guide You on the Higher Education Ladder of Success*, 170-180
Bensimon, Estela, and interviews of women's experiences, 80
Black for 31 Years: Nuances, 46-50
Black Issues in Higher Education, 79
  masters degree statistics and, 92
black women faculty
  and anchors for success, 159-167
  barriers facing and, 52
  and ideas for career advancement at PWIs, 52-53
  and obstacles in advancing academic careers, 157-167
Black Women in Academe, 51
Black Women in Higher Education: Negotiating the Cultural Workplace, 76-88
  academic affairs study, 79-81
  conclusion and recommendations, 87-88
  discussion of findings and, 85-86
  discussion of future research and, 86-87
  overview of literature and, 77-79
  and strategies used to negotiate the culture, 83-85
  study participants and, 81-83

professional background of, 214

Pippins, Shirley R., 234

Predominately White Institutions (PWIs), 182
  and different job descriptions for black females, 158
  and ideas for career advancement at, 52-53
  and primary challenges to faculty women of color, 97-110
  racism and, 48
  and social support networks, 69-70

Pregent, and guides for teaching excellence, 162

presidents, and Women of Color Presidents, 230-237

Presley, Vivian M., 234

Price, Glenda D., 182, 234
  challenges and, 37-38
  and role of dean, 36
  and *The Accidental President*, 35-39

professional conferences, seeking community support in, 106

Professional Organizations, seeking community support in, 105-106

professional relationships, importance of, 155

publishing
  tenure and research institutions, 150
  and tenure process, 145, 147, 161-162

R

race and gender stereotypes, 6-7, 52

racism
  and HBCU's and PWIs, 48
  and race and gender sterotypes, 52
  and standards for tenure, 136
  and survival strategies, 117-119

Ragster, LaVerne, professional background of, 215

Ragster, Laverne E., 234

Realities: This Mule Called My Back, 91-94

Reed, Trudie Kibbe, 182, 234
  and "internalized oppression", 40
  pathway to the presidency and, 42-45
  and presidential search committees, 43
  and *Road to the Presidency*, 40-45
  and spiritual leadership, 41-42

Reid-Wallace, Carolyn, 234

research institutions, and most widely used indicators for tenure, 150

Resources and Conference Information, 193-196
  American Association for Higher Education (AAHE), 193
  American Association of Community Colleges (AACC), 193
  American Association of State Colleges and Universities (AASCU), 193
  American Association of University Administrators (AAUP), 193
  American Association of University Professors (AAUP), 193

CONTRIBUTORS

AnnJanette Alejano-Steele is an associate professor in the departments of Psychology and Women's Studies at Metropolitan State College of Denver. Her educational background includes a Ph.D. in Developmental Psychology from Michigan State University and NIH-supported postdoctoral work in Psychology and Medicine from the University of California, San Francisco. She is committed to diversity issues in women's health, especially for women of color and is c urrently c onducting r esearch o n p sychosocial factors t hat a ffect birth outcomes for low-income African-American and Latina women. She is equally committed to diversity issues in higher education and curriculum, and she recently chaired the 7th annual Colorado Women of Color in Higher Education Conference in April, 2000. She is a co-facilitator for the Colorado Seeking Educational Equity and Diversity Project. She is equally committed to diversity issues in higher education and the K-college curriculum.

Carole Anderson holds a Ph.D. in Business Administration from Kent State University. She currently serves as Professor & Chair of the Department of Administrative Science at Clarion University of Pennsylvania. She has over 16 years of faculty experience, and has been published in journals such as the *Pennsylvania Journal of Business and Economics, Review of Business* and the *Journal of Professional Services Marketing.*

Conchita Y. Battle earned her Ed.D. in Higher Education A dministration from the University of Pennsylvania. With over 10 years of administrative experience in higher education, she has held administrative positions at Talladega College, Lincoln University [PA], and the University of Maryland College Park. She is currently the Director of the Advising Resource Center/EOP at California State University, Northridge and serves on the California Library Board.

Cheryl L. Clarke earned her Ph.D., M.A., and M.S.W. from Rutgers University, and her B.A. from Howard University. She has written several books of poetry. She has read her poetry and spoken at venues throughout the United States and served as member of the editorial collective for *Conditions* magazine. Clarke is the Director of the Office of Diverse Community Affairs and Lesbian-Gay Concerns at Rutgers, the State University of New Jersey-New Brunswick campus. Clarke also works on issues of diversity as well as issues of disabilities.

Beverly Anne Davis earned her Ph.D. in Social Work and Social Research from Bryn Mawr College. She is currently an Assistant Professor in Marywood University's School of Social Work. She has articles appearing in *Sage,* the *Journal of Teaching in Social Work, Child and Adolescent Social Work* and *Social Work.* She has made over thirty regional and national conference presentations about child welfare, race and social work training.

Brenda Sanders Dédé earned her Ed.D. in Higher Education Administration from Texas Southern University. She currently serves as Assistant Vice President for Academic Affairs at Clarion University of Pennsylvania with specific responsibility for research and graduate studies. She has served in administrative positions at Texas Southern University and Clarion for more than 20 years in addition to teaching part time at the University of Houston-Downtown, Houston Community College, and Texas Southern. She served on the American Association of State Colleges and Universities committee that produced the document "Facing Change: Building the Faculty of the Future".

Chontrese M. Doswell is the Associate Director for the Office of Graduate Recruitment, Retention and Diversity at the University of Maryland, College Park. Prior to her work in graduate education, she was an Assistant Professor in the departments of English, Philosophy and Modern Language, and Speech and Theater at Longwood College. She received the Ph.D. in Mass Communication from Howard University.

Dolores M. Fernández was named Interim President of Eugenio María de Hostos Community College of The City University of New York (CUNY) on March 1, 1998. She was appointed to the position of President effective July 1, 1999. Previously, Dr. Fernández had been a Professor of Curriculum and Teaching at Hunter College of CUNY; a Deputy Chancellor of Instruction and Development for the New York City Board of Education, and a Deputy Director for Program Services and a Director of Education with the New York State Division for Youth. After graduating cum laude from Nassau Community College, she earned a B.S. in Education from The State University of New York (SUNY) at Old Westbury, and an M.S. in Education as well as a Professional Diploma in Educational Administration from Long Island University (LIU)/C.W. Post College. She then earned her Professional Diploma in Reading and her Ph.D. in Language and Cognition from Hofstra University. Her academic honors include Title VII fellowships for both her M.S. and Ph.D. studies.

Joycelyn Finley-Hervey earned her Ph.D. in Organizational Behavior and Human Resource Management from the University of Michigan. She is an Associate Professor in the School of Business and Industry at Florida A&M University. Her research concentrates on intergroup relations and organizational dilemmas about value-laden issues associated with race, gender, and ethnicity. Dr. Finley-Hervey has contributed to several books and published in journals such as the African-American Research Perspectives and the Canadian Journal of Administrative Sciences.

Algeania Warren Freeman is the president of Livingstone College & Hood Theological Seminary in Salisbury, North Carolina. Dr. Freeman received her B.A. in English from Fayetteville State University, a M.A. degree in Speech Pathology & Audiology from Southern Illinois University, and her Doctorate Degree in Speech Communications from The Ohio State University. Dr. Freeman began her career in higher education as an Instructor at Norfolk State University and has held positions at Morgan State University, East Tennessee State University, Orange Coast College, and North Carolina AT&T University.

Cheryl Evans Green earned her Ph.D. in Social Work Administration, Policy and Planning from Clark Atlanta University. With over 23 years in the professoriate and 5 years as an administrator, she now serves as an Assistant professor in the School of Social Work, College of Health & Public Affairs at the University of Central Florida.

Sheila T. Gregory is an associate professor of higher education and educational leadership at Clark Atlanta University in Atlanta, GA. She holds a Ph.D. in higher education administration from the University of Pennsylvania. In the past decade, she has held faculty and/or administrative positions with the University of Pennsylvania, City University of New York, Kennesaw State University, University of Nevada-Las Vegas, the University of Memphis, Wayne State University and Clark Atlanta University. She is the author of 4 books, two books in progress, and nearly two dozen other scholarly publications that focus primarily on faculty and student recruitment and retention, professional leadership and development, and academic achievement with emphasis on race, ethnicity, class, and gender. In the past few years she has been awarded three Visiting Research Scholar Appointments with the American University in Cairo, Egypt, the University of South Australia, Adelaide, and the University of the West Indies System in Jamaica, Barbados, and Trinidad-Tobago and has consulted with numerous universities, community colleges, school districts, and tribal associations.

Judi Moore Latta (Ph.D., University of Maryland) is Professor and former Chair of the Department of Radio, TV, and Film at Howard University. Currently, she is Deputy General Manager of Howard University Television. As an award-winning producer of more than 70 radio documentaries, she is the recipient of the George Foster Peabody Award for her work as Senior Producer of the National Public Radio/Smithsonian Institution series "Wade in the Water: African American Sacred Music Traditions." She has also received production award recognition from the Corporation for Public Broadcasting, the American Women in Radio and TV, the National Education Association, the National Association of Black Journalists, and the National Federation of Community Broadcasters. Her research interests include cultural narratives and the politics of production.

Emma T. Lucas, Ph.D., LSW is professor of social work and chair, Division of Social Sciences at Carlow College. Dr. Lucas earned the Ph.D. and MSW at the University of Pittsburgh and a MA in Political Science from Purdue University. Prior to her current position, she was an associate vice president for academic affairs. Dr. Lucas received a National Institutes of Health grant to conduct research with Maternal Health Practices and Child Development Project at the University of Pittsburgh School of Medicine during the 1999-2000 academic year. Her research interests include social welfare and public policy issues that directly impact women and children, community organization, service-learning, and international social work. She is the author of a book and numerous articles. Dr. Lucas is also the president of the Pennsylvania Chapter-National Association of Social Workers.

Rebekah McCloud is the Assistant Director of the Office of Diversity Initiatives at the University of Central Florida. Dr. McCloud has earned a B.A. degree in Communications/Journalism, a M.Ed. degree in Educational Leadership, a M.S. degree in Business Management, and an Ed.D. degree in Curriculum and Instruction. She has accumulated over 25 years of service as an educator and professional journalist. Dr. McCloud has published articles, made many national presentations, designed workshops and facilitated training sessions. Her areas of expertise include recruitment and retention and leadership/career development. Former editor of the award-winning *Florida English Journal,* she reviews manuscripts for the *Journal of Adolescent & Adult Literature* a nd t he *Journal of Critical Inquiry Into Curriculum and Instruction.*

Deborah L. Owens earned her Ph.D in Human and Organizational Systems with an emphasis in Higher Education Administration from the Fielding Graduate Institute. She also holds an M.A. in Organizational D evelopment f rom Fielding a nd a n M .S. i n Child D evelopment from the University of California, Davis. Dr. Owens began her career in early childhood education/administration and has served as an administrator, college faculty, and consultant in this area for more than 20 years. Her research interests include women in higher education, leadership and management, organizational change and diversity issues.

Glenda D. Price is the President of Marygrove College in Detroit, Michigan. Dr. Price is the first lay woman and the first African American to be named president of Marygrove College. Prior to her presidency, Dr. Price served as Provost of Atlanta's Spelman College. Dr. Price holds a B.S. in medical technology, a M.Ed. in educational media and a Ph.D. in educational psychology from Temple University. She serves on several boards, including: Standard Federal, Alma College, New Detroit Inc., United Way Community Services, National Conference for Community and Justice, Detroit Executive Service Corps. and the Detroit Public School system.

Trudie Kibbe Reed is the 11th president of Philander Smith College of Little Rock, Arkansas. Dr. Reed is the first woman to serve in this capacity in the college's 125 years of history. In less than three years, President Reed brought all fund records in the 125 years by raising over $30 million dollars. Dr. Reed received B.A. and M.S.S.W. degrees from the University of Texas at Austin, and her M.A. and Doctorate Degree from Columbia University. Dr. Reed served 18 years as a senior level administrator with The United Methodist Church. At age 28, she became the youngest elected General Secretary CEO). She later served as an Associate General Secretary for the General Council on Ministries of The United Methodist Church. Dr. Reed was Director of The Leadership Institute and Professor of Education at Columbia College in Columbia, South Carolina where she founded and edited a refereed journal: "A Leadership Journal for Women: Women in Leadership - Sharing the Vision." While in South Carolina, Dr. Reed was recognized for outstanding leadership by the Governor, voted "Business Woman of the Year" and received the Diamond Twin Award from the YWCA. Dr. Reed has taught in the doctoral program at United Theological Seminary in Dayton, Ohio, and in the Master's Conflict Resolution program at Antioch University in Ohio.

Julie E. Stokes earned her Ph.D. in Psychology from the University of California, Riverside. She is an Associate professor in the Department of Afro-Ethnic Studies and Psychology at California State University, Fullerton, California. She teaches courses in The Psychology of African Americans, Black Women in America, the Black Family, the History of Racism, and Intercultural Socialization. She has published several book chapters on African American race socialization and Identity Development. She has several years experience serving as Chairperson for the San Bernardino County Mental Health Commission. Her research college students, racial and ethnic groups and genders. She has a strong commitment to the enterprise of teaching and to participant learning.

Anna L. Waring is an assistant professor in the Public Services Graduate Program at DePaul University. Waring teaches courses in management, the nonprofit sector, leadership, and policy analysis. Dr. Waring has been an administrator serving as Assistant Dean in the College of Liberal Arts and Sciences at DePaul University working on linking academics and community service opportunities and as a program officer for A Better Chance, Inc., a national educational organization. Dr. Waring received her doctorate in Administration and Policy Analysis from Stanford University's School of Education in 1995. Her research interests include leadership, administration and governance of colleges and universities, and community members' role in community policing in Chicago.

Evangeline A. Wheeler earned her Ph.D. in Cognitive Psychology from the University of California, Berkeley. As a tenured member of the faculty at Towson University, she holds the rank of Associate Professor in the Department of Psychology.

Gladys J. Willis earned her Ph.D. in English Literature from Princeton University. She was the first Black American to receive a Ph.D. in English from Princeton and was a Princeton scholar. She currently serves as Professor and Dean of Humanities and Graduate Studies at Lincoln University in Pennsylvania. She has over 30 years in a faculty rank and over 23 years of experience as an administrator in higher education.

Lynn Perry Wooten earned her Ph.D. from the University of Michigan. She holds the rank of Assistant Professor of Corporate Strategy at the University of Michigan Business School. Her general research area focuses on strategic human resource management and she has won awards from the McKinsey consulting firm, Academy of Management, and the Sloan Foundation. Professor Wooten is especially interested in research that examines the organizational challenges associated with employees balancing work and family. She has a paper in Sex Roles on this topic and a forthcoming book chapter in the Next Generation in Management Book Series published by the *Financial Times*.